BANANAS ABOUT MARKETING

Bananas About Marketing

HOW TO ATTRACT A WHOLE
BUNCH OF HAPPY CLIENTS

CHRISTO HALL AND FRANZISKA ISELI

Copyright © 2016 by Christo Hall and Franziska Iseli

All rights reserved. No part of this publication may be reproduced, stored in a retrieval system, or transmitted in any form or by any means, electronic, mechanical, photocopying, recording or otherwise, without prior written permission from the publisher.

National Library of Australia Cataloguing-in-Publication entry is available from the National Library of Australia Catalogue.

Calibri & Cambria fonts used with permission from Microsoft.

Edited by Wendy and Words (www.wendyandwords.com)

Text design and typesetting by Bookhouse (www.bookhouse.com.au)

Cover design by The Business Hood (www.thebusinesshood.com)

Illustrations by Paul Telling (www.paultelling.com.au)

ISBN: 978-1-63161-989-2

Published by TCK Publishing
www.TCKPublishing.com

Contents

Acknowledgements viii
Introduction ix

Part 1 **Your Marketing Foundations**

The story begins... 3
1 Vision and values 7
2 A success mindset 15
3 Creating your ideal lifestyle 25
4 Your ideal client 31
5 Positioning and branding 39
6 Building relationships 51

Part 2 **Kick-Butt Marketing Strategies to Attract More Clients and Grow Your Business**

7 Networking 67
8 Getting your website online 77
9 Social media 95
10 More online marketing strategies 115
11 Lumpy mail 131
12 The power of events and seminars 141
13 Teaming up 153
14 Copywriting that captivates 171
15 Advertisements 195

Part 3 **Communications and Sales** 203
16 Sales 205
17 Communication skills..229

Conclusion 243
Wait, there's more... 247
Bonus chapter from *The Modern Day Office*......................251
More products and programs by the authors...................263
About the authors..267
References 271

Disclaimer

ALL THE INFORMATION, TECHNIQUES, skills and concepts contained within this publication are of the nature of general comment only and are not in any way recommended as individual advice. The intent is to offer a variety of information to provide a wider range of choices now and in the future, recognising that we all have widely diverse circumstances and viewpoints. Should any reader choose to make use of the information contained herein, this is their decision, and the contributors (and their companies), authors and publishers do not assume any responsibility whatsoever under any conditions or circumstances. It is recommended that the reader obtain their own independent advice.

Acknowledgements

A HUGE 'THANK YOU' GOES TO OUR families who have always believed in us, even when we decided to travel the world while working and growing our business, supporting us no matter how crazy our ideas sounded. (Well, sometimes they probably just didn't know what we were up to).

We love you and truly appreciate you.

We would also like to thank our amazing clients. It is because of people like you we absolutely love what we do. We are so grateful to be able to work with so many incredible business owners and are passionate about supporting them to succeed and live the life of their dreams.

Thank you!
Franziska & Christo

Introduction

THANK YOU FOR TAKING ACTION towards your business success by acquiring a copy of *Bananas About Marketing*. The purpose of this book is to help small and micro business owners become great marketers of their own businesses so that they can attract more clients, make more money, live the lifestyle of their dreams, and ultimately contribute to society and make a difference.

A lot of people do not like marketing or have a negative emotion towards marketing and sales because it makes them think of sleazy sales people, brainwashing or companies that are trying to convince them to buy something they do not need. Well, that's not how we look at marketing, and it is definitely not the purpose of it. In this book we will show you how to market ethically and in line with your values. If you have a great product or service and people do not know about it, that is a shame. It is your job to get your fabulous product or service out there to the right people so that you can deliver value and improve the lives of others.

We would love you to enjoy marketing, as we do, rather than see it as something confusing, annoying or even bad. Marketing is like oxygen for your business—without it, your business cannot grow, let alone thrive. If you are in business (or about to start one) and want to make money to live your dreams and make a difference, the bottom line is you **need** to become good at marketing.

As you read this book, we invite you to think about how the ideas presented can apply to your own business. It's great to learn amazing new techniques and strategies, but even the greatest ideas are useless without being implemented. So at the end of each chapter we will give you specific action steps that will help you move forward.

The best way to maximise what this book offers is for you to implement one of the strategies covered in each chapter each month, exactly as outlined. Do this and within six months you will have set up a killer marketing machine that will be bringing in a continual flow of new and returning clients.

When you implement one strategy, make sure you do it well. Then test and measure and adjust before moving to the next one. We understand that it can be quite a challenge for a small business owner to find enough time to do all they need to, and that's why the last chapter, which is a BONUS CHAPTER, will introduce you to some strategies to free up your time.

People we work with often say that we make marketing so simple, doable and practical, and it is! In this book we have taken this concept to a whole new level. The sound marketing advice we share is entwined with an everyday story that illustrates and explains different marketing strategies in a very practical—and entertaining—manner. Each chapter begins with a snippet of the story of an Australian guy, Matt, and his search for the girl of his dreams, and how he finally hooks and keeps her. Through the story, you will not only find it easier to apply the lessons we share, but you will also thoroughly enjoy a good read!

For our international readers, we have added footnotes to explain the Aussie lingo to you! We are a Swiss/Aussie team who co-authored the book together, so you will find a good combination of Euro and Aussie imagery in our writing.

Bananas About Marketing is the fruit of countless hours of research and implementation of different marketing strategies—with many lessons of trial and error along the way—to enable us to share our gems of marketing wisdom with you. It is structured into three parts. In the first part you are going to discover how to **set the foundations right** for your business to grow. Then the second part will look at different innovative, practical and cost-effective **marketing strategies** to help you attract clients. The third part focuses on your **sales and communications skills** to help you increase your conversion rate.

This book is helping us to fulfill our mission to help small business owners worldwide live the life of their dreams. We truly believe it is a must-have resource for your business and marketing success kitbag.

So let's dive in and have fun!

Franziska & Christo

P.S. By the way, we would absolutely love your feedback. If you would like to share anything or have further questions after reading this book, please email *feedback@basicbananas.com*

PART 1

Your Marketing Foundations

Getting your act together before turning on the people magnet

The story begins...

I'VE HAD ENOUGH. I'VE TRIED EVERYTHING TO attract suitable girlfriends and I always get knocked back. I've spent so much money on flowers, going out to bars, shouting drinks for girls, and nothing has worked.

Matt was on his way home from another failed attempt to meet his dream woman at a pub near his workplace. He had spent the last two years trying to find a girlfriend and nothing seemed to work. He was in his early thirties and not a bad catch at all. He had a good job in an advertising agency as a client manager, and the best thing about it was six o'clock when the beer fridge magically opened, the amber fluid[1] started flowing and everyone still in the office got a drink or two. This did mean that they would stay even later because the alcohol would slow down their work, but

---

[1] 'Amber fluid' is another expression for beer, commonly used by bar flies, people who spends most of their time in a bar. Australians love their beer, and when you go to an Aussie pub, there are usually more beer brands on tap than people in the bar.

Matt didn't mind hanging out at the agency. He didn't have anybody to go home to anyway—though that was starting to get to him.

One late night, a few beers down, Matt started talking to Fabio, a creative director in his late forties. Matt lamented about his dilemma with women and that he just can't seem to attract the right one. The alcohol made him open up more and the words flowed like beer at beer o'clock.

Fabio burst out laughing, "Mate, I've been there and had to learn a few things along the way, and now I'm in a loving relationship with my wife and our two gorgeous kids. You know, this may sound weird, and I'm not some sort of love guru, but if you want, I can help you out with some stuff. I seriously made so many mistakes when I was your age, and it would be my pleasure to share them with you to make sure your journey to finding the amore of your life is more enjoyable than mine was!" With an elegant hand movement, Fabio pushed his long dark hair back and smiled at Matt.

With a glint of hope in his eyes, Matt looked up from his third bottle of beer and smiled an innocent smile. "Really, you would do that? That would be insane. I've seen you with your lady and you seem such a perfect match."

"Hmmm, yes we are! Okay, let's do it. Before we get into some powerful methods of influence that will surely have the ladies lining up to know you, let's have a look at some of the basic stuff you need to know. Without these foundations, you'll be building your relationships on slippery slopes."

The story begins... 5

Matt walked over to the beer fridge, handed Fabio a cold bottle of VB[2]—unfortunately the agency was on a budget—grabbed a chair and sat down on it backwards, his arms resting on the back. He was all ears.

Without meaning for it to happen consciously, Matt had just made one of the biggest steps towards his success. He had found himself a mentor, someone to learn from who has experienced the success he desires. Unfortunately, a lot of business owners will rarely ask for help or seek a course or program that will accelerate their results.

One of the first rules to business growth and success is to find a mentor or program that will teach you things you do not know and will help you grow your business. The majority of highly successful people have an open attitude to learning and select the right expert to help them achieve their goals in any given area.

---

[2] Victoria Bitter beer, also known as 'Vitamin B,' a common beer found in virtually every pub in Australia.

1

Vision and values

Keep your dream alive and be true to yourself

"People only see what they are prepared to see."

~ RALPH WALDO EMERSON

"FIRST OF ALL, WE'RE GOING TO START WITH THE very basics. you need to have a vision and goals to get you to where you want to be in, say, five or ten or even twenty years' time. Have you ever heard the saying, 'If you don't have a goal, you will never get there?'" Fabio looked at Matt to see his reaction.

"Yep, I totally get it. Well, in ten years I'd like to be married to a gorgeous and intelligent woman, have two, maybe three, children and live in our own house on the beach in Sydney."

"Sounds good. Okay. For today, I'm just going to give you one task. Write that down and stick it up on your bathroom mirror so you see it every day. Lesson over for today." And with that Fabio sat back and enjoyed his beer.

That night Matt wrote down his goal and added a few more for good measure. He put them on the bathroom mirror (after cleaning it first, of course, as Matt was a bit of a neat freak). He wasn't too sure about this whole idea but he thought, Why not? He hadn't been very successful so far and it wouldn't hurt.

Why do we talk about vision in this book? It's a book about marketing, right? **Your business vision is your driver, your motivator and your big reason for being in business in the first place.** (Unless of course someone forced you to be in business or you inherited one!) It is your vision that will help you and your team stay motivated and on track when things get tough.

Your vision will also direct your marketing strategies. Knowing where you want to go will help you choose and implement the right strategies to get you there.

What is your vision for your business? Is it to save the world? To be the number one cleaning business in Sydney helping people live bacteria-free? To help one million people live a healthy life? To minimise illiteracy in the world by providing reading courses accessible to underprivileged children? To be rated as a five-star restaurant providing an extraordinary dining experience?

Once you are clear about where you want your business to go, share your vision with your team members and put it on your website and other marketing materials for your prospects to see. Your vision will not only inspire yourself and your team, but will also inspire clients and prospects to do business with you.

If you wake up unmotivated in the morning, hitting the snooze button five times, then try putting a piece of paper with your vision on your bedside table. It will help you get out of bed. Here is the thing—if you find it hard to get up in the morning, either you are partying too much and staying up too late or you do not have a big enough reason and purpose for being in business. If your reason for being in business is just to pay your bills and get by, you might not feel very motivated. If it is because you want to make a difference, have freedom and spend time with your family every day, you will be more motivated.

We will share with you our vision at Basic Bananas as an example. Reminding ourselves of our vision every day keeps us motivated and on track:

> *To be the number one marketing support system for business owners worldwide. We want every small business owner to have access to our valuable marketing resources to support the business and life they desire. We believe that happy and successful people give back to the community and can all make a difference through social business. We are out to change the world one business owner at a time.*

The next day, Matt and Fabio met up in the staff room for coffee. "Let's take it one step further, Matt. You've done really well with your vision. Now let's look at your values! This next task will really help you be congruent with yourself, and you will find it much easier to make decisions. It will certainly also help you choose the right ladies or say no to the ones that don't fit in with your values." Fabio nodded in agreement with his own ideas.

"Hmmm. Sounds intriguing. I've never really thought of it that way. I kind of understand the concept, but I'm not sure how to apply it to my life. How do I determine my values? I have no clue what my values are." Matt was scratching his head, and his usually neat hair now looked a bit messy.

"Easy. All you need to do is ask yourself what's important in your life, in your relationships and in your career. Brainstorm everything that comes to mind and don't stop until you have a good list of values. Let me give you a few examples of possible values: love, family, wealth, health, freedom, satisfaction, happiness... There are hundreds of them."

Matt was already armed with pen and paper, ready to go.

Your business values are crucial. Not only will they help you make decisions, they will also allow your prospects to know what they can expect when working with you. For our own business and our clients' businesses, being clear about the values the business stands for has been invaluable. It has certainly also helped with decision-making processes. We remember one specific situation when a guy wanted to work with us and signed up to one of our small business marketing programs. But after finding out more about him and his business, we had to say no to him because we would have had to compromise on our value of integrity. His way of doing business was not in line with how we do business, and it would have been hard to change that.

Once you are clear on your values, a great idea is to always keep them handy so that you and your team members are reminded of what is most important to your business and can set priorities accordingly. Some larger businesses insist that their team members carry a card with the company values on it at all times when at work. When an employee shows their commitment to one of the business's values, they get rewarded for it. They understand the power of having values and standing by them.

It is the values in your business that will differentiate you from your competitors and make your clients stick with you as they know exactly what they get when working with you.

It's your turn to take action

Take a few minutes right now to think about and write down what your business vision is. Put it up on your website and your marketing materials, and post it around the office for your staff to see. And don't forget to put it on your bedside table. (You might even impress your partner or prospective partner).

Now let's determine your business values.

Step 1: Answer the question—"What is important in my business?" Write down all the things that pop into your mind. Do not de-select anything yet; just keep writing. The best ones often come at the end when you think that there are no more. This is a brain dump exercise.

To get you started, here are some examples of business values:

Leadership, flexibility, quality, customer service, integrity, knowledge, excellence, health, freedom, care, fun, creativity, wisdom, variety, honesty

Step 2: Now prioritise them. Which ones are more important than others? Ask yourself questions like, "Is integrity more important than customer service?" And keep comparing your values until you have your values in order of priority. In this step, you also start weeding out some of your less important values.

Step 3: Now select the top 5 – 7 values and adopt them for your business.

Step 4: Put them on your marketing materials, on your website and around your office for everyone to see, and make sure your business lives by them every day. Do not compromise or you won't feel very good.

2

A success mindset

Is your stubby³ half full or half empty?

"A person who never made a mistake never tried anything new."

~ ALBERT EINSTEIN

"FABIO, DO YOU HAVE A SECOND?" MATT WAS smiling from ear to ear.

"Yes, of course!" Fabio got up from his desk where he had scraps of paper, brochures and pens all over the place, living up to his image of being a messy creative.

---

³ A stubby is a short 375 ml glass bottle used for beer. Not to be confused with stubby shorts, which are skimpy, and sometimes indecent, shorts worn by Aussie men in summer—not very sexy.

"You know what happened last night? Of course you don't... but I'm sure you can guess... No, I didn't meet my dream girl... but I did do the values exercise you gave me and got really clear on my values; it took me about forty-five minutes. Then something happened; it suddenly dawned on me why I wasn't fulfilled in my last relationship even though the girl was great!" Matt was excited by his realisation.

"This whole values thing is great, isn't it?" said Fabio, as calm as always.

"Man, it is! The reason why I wasn't completely happy in my last relationship was because one of my top values is freedom, which clearly wasn't fulfilled in that relationship because my girl wanted to do everything together and didn't give me the space I needed. Now I understand why it's important to know my values because when they aren't respected, I don't feel happy and satisfied. Wow, meaningful stuff, Fabio! Don't tell anyone I'm getting into this deep' n meaningful new age stuff, will you, mate? Otherwise my workmates will think that I've gone troppo[4]!

"Anyway," Matt continued, "I know you are busy, Fabio, but I just wanted to share this with you. I am so excited. This is going to help me in many areas of my life, not only in relationships."

"You're a quick learner, Matt." Fabio gave Matt a big pat on the back. "I'm busy today, but tomorrow I will show you something else that will blow your mind."

---

[4] 'Gone troppo' means to have gone crazy and lost the veneer of civilisation after spending too long in the tropics).

"I can't wait! I'll shout[5] you lunch. 12.30 in the foyer?"

"Deal."

Matt was already waiting in the foyer at 12.20 pm as he was eager to learn more and get moving on his journey to attracting more ladies.

"Hey, mate; let's go down to the pub. They've got some great steaks," Fabio suggested. As they were waiting for their meals, Fabio started his lecture. "Okay, Matt. This is one of the most important lessons I'm going to teach you, although I'll probably say 'this is the most important lesson' a few times. I've got so much more in store for you."

"I'm ready!" Matt got a pen and paper out of his man-bag, like a nerdy school boy ready to write an essay.

"Do you know the number one reason why people fail in relationships, business, careers, sports... in any area?" Fabio looked at Matt who was sitting with a straight back and pen poised.

"No idea, Fabio. Talent? Or is it money? You can buy everything with money." He said this second one half-jokingly as he smiled, guessing the answer wasn't really going to be money.

"Yes and no." Fabio's dark eyes started wandering around the pub. "Talent obviously helps, but it is usually not the defining ingredient." He pointed at a waitress across the room that was balancing three big plates and continued. "This lady definitely has talent

---

[5] To shout someone lunch has got nothing to do with yelling. It means to pay for something for somebody, commonly used for drinks at a pub. "I'll shout you a drink" or "It's my shout."

when it comes to waitressing, but does she have what it takes to be the head waitress in an exclusive, upper-class, fine dining restaurant where she'd be getting paid more in tips than you make in your advertising job? What really makes the difference is...," Fabio paused for impact and took a sip of his cold beer, "...mindset."

"What kind of a word is that? Mindset... did you make that up?" Matt looked a little disappointed; he was waiting for a big reveal.

"Okay, let me explain. Mindset is everything when it comes to success in any area of your life. You see people who take action and are committed to something get results—there's no two ways about it. Those people that sometimes make a bit of a mistake but keep trying, even when they get a knock back, are the true champions. The problem comes when people don't believe in themselves and give up too early or, even worse, they imagine what could go wrong before they even give something a go. Most people are geniuses at imagining everything that could go wrong, which causes them to fear the embarrassment that would come from a failure. This is usually enough to stop them from taking action and going for it. Their thoughts are playing like a movie in their heads over and over again.

"So, things like asking a girl on a date or making sales calls at work or pitching for new jobs just seem not 'doable.' Of course it's more comfortable to do things with less risk involved and with less chance of a knock back. And once again, our genius mind goes to work and finds other tasks for us to do that keep us safe. Let me give you a practical example you'll understand. Imagine a high school student who has never cleaned his bedroom suddenly feels the urge to do so right before he has to study for an end-of-year exam. Why? Because it's uncomfortable to study and tidying up keeps him in the comfort zone."

Fabio realised that Matt, who had been frantically taking notes, suddenly stopped and looked up. "You following, Matt?"

"Yeah, Fabio. I know this all too well. I think the penny kind of dropped."

"You see Matt, we've all got a little voice inside our head that's there to protect us from potential embarrassment, from risk and also from the rewards that come from taking risks." Fabio tapped the side of his head to make his point clearer.

"I know what you mean," said Matt with a pained expression. "I'm usually pretty confident when approaching new girls, but when I really like one, I get sweaty palms and my heart races just thinking about asking her out and embarrassing myself if she says no. Your lesson today is totally hitting home, Fabio." Matt paused for a second. "I play a little mind movie, imagining everything that could go wrong."

"Exactamente!" responded Fabio with a big smile and loud enough for most people in the pub to hear. For a moment, Matt admired Fabio's perfectly white teeth. How can they be so perfect, like miniature piano keys... but without the black keys...

Matt shook his head as if to get himself back on topic. "I understand that my fear could make me miss out on potential opportunities. But what can I do about it?" Matt asked. "I get nervous when I'm leaving my comfort zone, and to be honest I probably don't even believe in myself!"

"Don't worry, mate. I've got five tips for you that I was taught by a master yogi." Fabio looked at Matt, wondering whether he was ready for such knowledge. "Well, he's not really a master yogi. My friend Jonesy did all these personal development courses and thinks he's a bit of a guru now. But anyway, his tips are beauties[6] and have worked well for me. Are you ready?"

Matt nodded eagerly and Fabio continued. "Okay, here are Jonesy's 5 Tips...

Jonesy's 5 tips to overcome fear and take action

1. When you are faced with a situation that makes you nervous, ask yourself, "What's the worst that can happen if I continue?" If your answer is "Nothing" or "Nothing life changing," then do it.
2. Acknowledge the little heroic protector that is the voice inside your head. As soon as you acknowledge the voice, instead of trying to ignore it, it will disappear. You can even give it a name to make it more interesting. Thank him or her for trying to protect you and let it go. "Thank you for trying to protect me, Rod, but I'm doing it anyway, and I'll be fine."

---

[6] Another Aussie slang word, meaning something great or fantastic.

3. Focus on what you want and imagine what it's like to have it. This will help you keep on track and become less distracted in achieving your outcome. When you start a task, do it to completion.
4. Focus on what you need to do next to achieve your desired outcome. When we beat ourselves up, our focus is on ourselves. And when we are growing or moving forward, our focus is on others or our environment or the next step.
5. Finally, my favourite: Celebrate your success when you overcome something that scares you, when you have achieved a great result despite having been scared at the beginning. Reward yourself for having stepped outside of your comfort zone."

"Jonesy is a genius." Matt's look of concern had turned into confidence; he was ready to take action.

"What the heck is mindset?" you might ask! According to thesaurus.com, mindset is a habitual or characteristic mental attitude that determines how you will interpret and respond to situations.

The bad news is that your mindset plays a huge role in your business success. The good news is that your mindset is not part of your identity and is changeable.

To develop a success mindset you need to have a clear goal of what you want to achieve and then have complete focus on getting there. What gets you there is taking action, determination and discipline. Et voila, you are on your way to developing your success mindset and achieving more than you would ever have dreamt of.

Use Jonesy's tips above to overcome nerves and acknowledge the little voice inside your head that will no doubt pop up, whether it's to ask for business from a potential client or meet new people at a networking event. 'Feel the fear and do it anyway' as Susan Jeffers writes in her book with the same title. Every time you are doing something that pushes you out of your comfort zone, you are growing. So **welcome a good challenge**, as it is presenting you with an opportunity to grow.

Often business owners, particularly start-up businesses, are looking for motivation and searching for something or someone to inspire them that are fabulous. You can also find motivation by challenging yourself and stepping outside your comfort zone. Think about the last time you felt really motivated, and then think of what happened immediately before you felt that motivation. More than likely you challenged yourself in some way or you overcame something that made you feel uncomfortable.

Yes, this book is about marketing, but if your mindset isn't set for success, no marketing strategy will work for you.

> ### It's your turn to take action
>
> Kick yourself in the butt to do something(s) that will give your business a boost. Think about three things you know you could do that would be good for your business but so far have scared you a little—but so much so that you have put them off for a long time! Write down those three things now and commit to doing them, one after the other.
>
> By taking this action you will gain motivation that will work like fuel for you to take the next step.
>
> The more times you stretch yourself, the more motivation you will gain. It's like rolling a snowball down a snowy hill in the Swiss mountains; the more you get the ball rolling, the bigger and faster it will go—just make sure you do not cause an unmanageable avalanche!

3

Creating your ideal lifestyle

Time to fantasise!

"If you can dream it, you can do it."

WALT DISNEY

"LET'S HAVE SOME FUN NOW MATT! THIS IS ONE of the most important lessons I'm ever going to teach you. Okay, I said that yesterday, didn't I? I told you there will be many more 'most important' lessons. It might sound a bit fluffy, but just go with it and you'll see. This stuff actually works. In fact, the first time I ever heard of this was from Frank Kern, an online marketing guru. Although I usually run for the hills[7] as fast as I can when I hear the word 'guru,' his results were amazing. And I'm sure he wasn't the first one to do this. In fact most successful entrepreneurs know the power of visualising their goals.

"This is what Frank Kern did. He wrote down exactly what his ideal life would look like, including where he would live, what he would be doing all day, who he would be working with, how much money he would be making and even how his ideal house would look. Only a few years later, he realised that he had pretty much achieved everything he wrote down, including details such as a big shower with two showerheads! Fascinating, hey?"

Fabio started drifting off again; he was known for entering his own 'dream world' at times. Then quick as a flash, he looked Matt straight in the eyes and pointed his finger at him. "This is what I want you to do, Matt: Take thirty minutes tonight when you get home (no beers after work), sit down in your favourite spot with a pen and paper and your favourite music in the background, and then start writing down how your ideal day and life would look like—exactly how you would like your average day, every day, to be like. Answer questions such as: What are you eating for breakfast? Who with? What are you doing in the morning? What are you doing for work? What are you having for lunch? What sort of discussions do you have with your friends? Who are your friends? How are your relationships? What are your hobbies? Where do

---

[7] To run for the hills is an Australian expression for running away from something. It's easier to run for the hills, rather than face something that is annoying, isn't it?

you live? How is your girlfriend? Etcetera, etcetera. You get the point, right?"

"This does sound a bit weird," replied Matt, "but hey, I thought the values thing was weird and it was absolutely magic. I'm gonna give this thing a go. So, all I do is write down exactly what a perfect day would look like for me? I've never really thought about it before."

"I then want you to save your answers," continued Fabio. "Put them somewhere safe. In a few years' time, look at them again and you will be surprised how much you've achieved! What has this got to do with getting a girlfriend? A lot! You need to have your own life in order first, be happy with yourself and know exactly what you want in life before you can attract the right girl. It's as simple as that. Your own happiness doesn't depend on anyone but you."

Unfortunately, so many small business owners live far from their ideal life or ideal work day. What started out as a dream of freedom and flexibility as a business owner turned into 16-hour work days and less money in the bank than ever before. We are on a mission to change this and help business owners realise their dreams—**the reasons why they first set out in business.**

Those dreams—your ideas and goals—have to be articulated. To be able to live your ideal life, each and every day, you first need to know what you want and what it would look like. It's similar to doing research on the internet about your next holiday. Do you want beaches or mountains? Do you want to stay in a five-star hotel or at the campground? If you do not know what you want, you might not find anything. The clearer you are about your perfect holiday, the higher the probability that you will end up having it.

The exercise that Fabio instructed Matt to complete is very important. If you don't think so now, you will in a few years' time when you take your piece of paper out of the bottom of a drawer and tick off all the things you have achieved. We are the living proof of this. To be honest, when we first did this exercise a few years ago, we were not so sure about its impact and whether it's just garbage. But within less than a year we have managed to live our ideal day almost every day, including living in our own beachfront apartment, going surfing or taking a walk on the beach every day. We are travelling around the world while working and growing our business, working with our ideal clients, having a book published and eating a good meal for dinner at night instead of cereal. (That last one might sound very simple for you, but it wasn't very easy for two people who would rather read a book, play music or go surfing than cooking).

Here is proof of a little note Christo put on the wall of his office in 2006.

> Own businesses – which I don't need to be physically in one place.
>
> Beach House
>
> Speak German – Swiss
>
> Surf & Travel
>
> Monkey
>
> Play Music

Christo: I wrote these goals in 2006 and within a couple of years, I pretty much had achieved all of them. I created a business that allows me and Franziska to work from anywhere, we bought a beach apartment, I learnt to speak Swiss-German (although that one is still a work in progress!), I surf and travel whenever I like to, I got married to my monkey (Franziska) and we play a lot of music.

We wanted to share this with you to inspire you to dream and write down your goals and you will no doubt achieve them.

It's your turn to take action

Put this book down for twenty minutes and ask yourself, "How exactly would my ideal life and day look?" Write down every detail. You can also refer back to the storyline above for some ideas. Where do you live? What are you doing all day? Who are you working with? How much money are you making? Who are your friends? How does your ideal house look? Putting on your favourite music might help to stimulate your brain too. (Ok, maybe not if it's heavy metal).

After you've completed this exercise, put your list in a safe place and then, in about twelve months' time, go back to it and check off what you have accomplished. You will be surprised!

4

Your ideal client

The dream date

"The odds of hitting your target go up dramatically when you aim at it."

~ UNKNOWN

THE NEXT DAY, FABIO AND MATT MET FOR LUNCH again at the local pub, a wannabe Irish pub with nothing that resembled Ireland except for green bar stools and a couple of Irish posters which, all in all, were enough to get the placed filled on St. Patrick's Day.

"Fabio, I took thirty minutes to write everything about my ideal day and ended up with four pages of handwritten notes! I'm still not sure I believe in it, but it felt really good anyway. A lot of things have become clear to me, including what kind of girl I would like to call my own."

"That's fabulous, Matt, because that's exactly what I want to work on with you today. I think you are now ready to attract the right girl... or girls. Remember, having the right foundations will make everything come so much easier. We've got forty-five minutes and then I need to be back for an important pitch at Credit Suisse. I'm hoping to get some business out of those Swiss bankers. Could potentially be a huge job for our small advertising agency and finally a pay rise for Don Fabio."

Fabio took a big sip of his diet coke and muttered, "I'm starving. I wonder if they had to go and kill a cow to make my steak. Every time I come to this pub the service is so slow, even though I tell them that we are in a hurry. That's a problem a lot of businesses have, you know; they don't listen to their customers. This pub is almost empty, and it could be full every day, not just on St. Patrick's Day, with advertising agency people if only the service was a bit faster. We don't have all day to sit here and scratch ourselves." Fabio seemed a bit grumpy, but he still managed to smile across the table where Matt was sitting armed with his usual pen and paper.

"You know, Matt," Fabio continued, "this is part of the lesson I want to teach you today—knowing your target or ideal market, or in your case, your ideal girl.

"Now that you know your ideal, perfect day, you are ready to look at your ideal 'client' or girl to fit in with your ideal life, in that order. Wouldn't it be annoying if you got a girl and then tried to change yourself to make it work? I think the relationship is much more sustainable and more likely to survive if you first get clear on how you would like to live, and then attract the right girl... a girl who wants you for who you are and not for who she wants you to become. Of course, you will create your ideal life together, but it helps knowing what you want."

Matt nodded as he was taking notes. "Absolutely. I reckon I would set myself up for disaster if I found the perfect girl that might not fit in with my ideal life or tried to change who I am. After a few years, the perfect girl might not be so perfect anymore, and I would have to start again from scratch, still not living my ideal day."

"Exactamente!" Fabio put on his Italian accent as he nodded, his black ponytail bobbing up and down. "Let's get you working then! What I want you to do is describe every detail of your ideal girl. Answer the following questions: How old?... Where does she live?... How does she look?... What is she like?... What does she do for work?... What are her hobbies?... What does she read?... Where does she hang out?... What are her secret desires?... What are her frustrations?... You can even give her a name."

"So I'm pretty much creating my dream girl, is that right? And I assume your reasoning is that if I know who I want to attract into my life, she will just appear, out of the blue." Matt was a tad sarcastic.

"Well, not exactly. You still need to do some work to get her. It's not like kissing a frog and your princess miraculously appears; after all you're not living a fairy tale. But when you know where she might hang out, what she loves and what her hobbies are, your chances of finding her are much higher."

"Got it!" Matt nodded and started writing again.

"Molto bene! And here is my steak. I've got five minutes to devour it, three minutes too long." Fabio picked up his knife and fork and started attacking his steak like a seagull that's just nicked a hot chip from a surprised tourist at Bondi Beach[8].

"See you on Friday after work for a vino and your next important lesson. Tomorrow I'm busy."

"Sounds great. Thank you, Fabio. I really appreciate being your 'apprentice.'"

"You are welcome, mate. I love working with action takers!" Fabio grabbed the bill and walked up to the counter to pay.

Without really knowing and understanding your ideal client, you might as well chuck[9] your marketing money out of the window or spend it on lollies.

Defining, researching and understanding your ideal client is what we usually make our clients do first, and a lot of them do not like it because it's something unfamiliar. But once they get into it, they

---

[8] Bondi Beach is the closest beach to Sydney and very popular. On a hot summer's day Bondi Beach is packed with sunbaking tourists and Aussies looking like sausages on a BBQ.

[9] 'To chuck' something means to throw something. For example 'I chucked the sausage away because it was burned.' Or 'to chuck a wobbly' means to throw a tantrum.

love it, and the results they get after really understanding their ideal client speak for themselves.

The better you know your ideal client, the better you will be able to service them, target them and give them what they want. Your aim is to know them better than your competitors; do that and you will never run out of business.

Sounds pretty easy, right? Well, it is pretty easy, but still a majority of businesses do not know their target market and spend thousands of dollars on marketing techniques that do not work.

Not only will knowing your target market help you find them, instead of having a hit-and-miss approach to marketing where you just hope that somebody will come or see your advertisement, it will also help you direct your marketing materials more specifically to them. You will be able to write and talk directly to them rather than to everybody. If your marketing is targeting everybody, nobody will listen. If your marketing is targeting a specific person or group of people, they will feel as if they are being spoken to directly and will listen. They will realise that you are the one that understands what they want and need better than anybody else, and probably even better than they themselves do.

Let's illustrate this with a practical example. If you have a business selling baby food, you could target everybody because mums, dads, grandmas, grandpas, sisters, brothers... they could all be potential buyers. Or you could target mums only and speak to their core needs and wants by talking about what a great supplement this food is in terms of benefits to mums: their babies will grow strong and be healthy; it will save time to prepare **because you understand** how busy mums are and how their baby will love the taste of the healthy food. You are speaking in terms of benefits to the mums. By doing so, you gain their attention and give them a feeling of "Ah yes. They understand me".

You could be even more specific and target mums with babies that don't sleep very well if that is the problem your product is solving. Put that on your marketing material and suddenly you will have the attention of a specific group of mums.

Why do businesses not do exactly that then—narrow in on a specific target market? Because they are scared that they will miss out on potential buyers. Wrong! It won't mean that dads won't buy the baby food as well, they will still buy it. But at least somebody will take notice of your marketing material and find it easier to remember your product and tell their friends about it.

Let's take this even further. If you have two completely different markets, say you are a mindset coach and your market is sports people and also business owners, then you would have two completely different marketing approaches rather than mixing the two target markets—because their needs and wants are completely different. You would have different marketing materials for each market and use different strategies to get their attention.

The cool thing is that it is up to you to choose who you want to work with. We have done this exercise with hundreds of business owners, and it is quite interesting how they started attracting more of their ideal clients and less of the ones they do not want to work with. As a little side note here, once you know who you want to work with, it will also make it easier for you to say no to clients and customers that cost you more than they are of benefit, taking you away from your great clients and customers.

But how do you get to know your ideal client and find out what they want?... Ask them!

One of the best ways to understanding your clients and what they want is to ask them to fill in a short survey that asks questions such as:

What would make our services or products even more outstanding?

- *What do/don't you like about our business?*
- *What would be one thing we could improve on?*
- *What is your biggest frustration in relation to <product or service>?*
- *What do you like most about <product or service>?*

A great, free online survey tool is SurveyMonkey:

www.surveymonkey.com

> ### It's Your Turn to Take Action
>
> 1. **Determine who you ideal client is:** Narrow down your target market and decide who your ideal client is. (No, it's not everybody!)
> 2. **Do some research on your ideal client:** Create a survey and ask questions such as those as outlined above. Find out what their desires and frustrations are, where they live, where they hang out, how old they are, what they do for work etc. You will most likely get priceless feedback that will not only help you provide an even better service or product to your market but will also help you market and sell them.
> 3. **Describe your ideal client in detail:** Now that you have chosen and researched your ideal client, describe them in every detail so that you can keep them in mind when marketing to them.

In *Chapter 14 Copywriting that Captivates*, we will go into even more detail about how to research your target market.

5

Positioning and branding

Turn up your mojo

"I am not looking like Armani today and somebody else tomorrow. I look like Ralph Lauren. And my goal is to constantly move in fashion and move in style without giving up what I am."

~ RALPH LAUREN

"MATT, I FORGOT TO MENTION SOMETHING yesterday, and I want you to learn about this before tomorrow when we look at one of the most important marketing... um, dating... principles. I will give you a quick run-down, and then you can go away and think about it and ask me questions tomorrow." Fabio sat on the edge of Matt's desk where Matt was busy updating his Facebook status.

"I'm all ears. Just...," Matt lowered his voice as he quickly got up to close the door, "... I don't want my workmates to know that I am such a beginner when it comes to girls." Matt grimaced.

"Matt, you are no beginner, mate. You are just doing what most people are doing, getting the same ordinary results, doing the same ordinary things. I'm only giving you some little tips and tricks that will improve your results; you're the one that's taking action." Fabio looked out of the window, pointing at a tree. "See that tree over there?"

"Yes," Matt replied, slightly confused.

"It's a beautiful tree, isn't it? It's been looked after by the council for the last... I don't know how many years. And now it's huge and healthy. With the right ingredients, this tree grew into a magnificent tree. It would still be a wonderful tree without having been looked after, but the extra ingredients made it grow even bigger, better and more healthy."

"I see what you're getting at... I think. Right now I am an average tree, and maybe once I've learnt and applied all the concepts you are teaching me, I will become a fabulous tree... right?" Matt still looked a bit confused, but just went with it, knowing that Fabio is known to drift off into weirdo land.

Fabio snapped back into reality and checked his watch. "Only got five minutes to teach you something—just enough time. Remember how we spoke about how important it is to think about who you want to attract? Well, what I forgot to add is that you also need to know how you want to be perceived. Have you ever heard of 'personal branding?'"

"Personal branding? Yeah, I might have heard some of our PR chicks talk about it, but I always thought it was bull[10]." Matt clicked off the Facebook page and typed 'Personal Branding' into Google Search. "I thought I was ready to get out there and meet some girls!"

"Almost Matt, almost. The next step to be successful in attracting the right girls is to look at your personal branding. Your branding has to be a match to what you want to achieve in life and to your ideal girls, otherwise you'll attract the wrong ones and for sure you'll never end up in a serious relationship... with the right girl"

Fabio looked at Matt, took a deep breath and added, "You look a bit confused mate. Let me give you an example. If you aspired to become the CEO of this company, you wouldn't walk around in trackie dacks[11] because no one would take you seriously. You'd make sure your personal brand and actions reflect those of an aspiring CEO. Makes sense?"

Matt nodded as Fabio continued. "Okay, then. You know there is a lot of competition nowadays; lots of other guys are chasing the same type of girls you like. So you need to stand out and be the number one choice. There are a few rules you need to follow to be successful, such as being consistent, delivering on your promises, building trust and standing for something. I know that sounds like an awful lot of stuff to consider.

---

[10] Bull: short for bull cr#p or bull s#*t, meaning nonsense.
[11] Trackie dacks: tracksuit pants in the Aussie language.

Let's get started with the basics. Think about your image; how do you want to be perceived?"

"I guess I want to be seen as fun, intelligent, loyal and stylish. Oh, and sexy would be good too." Matt had a huge smile on his face, thinking about his own ideal characteristics.

"Hmmm... stylish? You've got a long way to go, mate. But that's okay. We'll get you there. I might have to take you shopping." Fabio laughed out loud and Matt joined in, looking down at his skinny pants and converse shoes.

The purpose of business branding nowadays is not only to sell a product or service, but also to sell an experience, a feeling, a lifestyle, a meaning and a sense of belonging. We are living in a world of abundance and people do not always buy stuff because of its practicality, but because it feels or looks good. Often we want to be associated with the lifestyle that comes with the brand.

Why would you buy a BMW rather than a Hyundai? Or why would you buy Gucci sunglasses rather than an unknown brand? Because of the image the brand has managed to build. Buying fancy sunnies or an expensive car makes you feel good, and it also says something about your status. It determines the way people perceive you.

Your business brand is much more than just a logo or a flyer; it is your business identity and personality.

Apple® computers are a fabulous example of excellent branding! They sell 'being different, belonging to a certain creative tribe and style' rather than the products themselves. So, every time they bring out a new product, their customers can't wait to buy it. They have managed to create an amazing brand with millions of followers.

Let's look at a few things you can do to create a desirable brand.

Be consistent

So the first thing you need to do is to think about what you want your brand to stand for. Do you want your brand to be perceived as expensive, professional, cheeky, cheap, unique, elegant or funny? Once you have determined your brand's personality, make sure the images you use, your font, your tone of voice, your colours, your designs, and so on are consistent across all applications.

Consistency in fact is a huge factor in your branding success. Besides being consistent with your look and feel, it is also important to be consistent in the delivery of your services and products. If you fail to be consistent in your delivery, you will lose repeat customers, and they will be less likely to refer you to their friends, family and colleagues.

Imagine, for example, going to your local hairdresser and on your first visit she does a fabulous job, but next time you walk out looking like you have just been through an experiment. You probably would not go back there and you also would not recommend her, which is a shame because she might be a fabulous hairdresser—but her delivery of service is very inconsistent. Or you go to the local pie shop[12] and one day the lady remembers your name and is super friendly and the next she is short and grumpy for no reason (unless you have forgotten to tell her how gorgeous her new haircut is).

Consistency evokes familiarity and familiarity leads to more sales, full stop.

Provide excellent customer service

Customer service is something every brand can excel in; but unfortunately a lot of businesses do not spend a minute on increasing the quality of their customer service. Has it ever happened to you that you walk into a shop and the shop assistant behind the counter is chatting on the mobile phone, looking at you with an expression that says 'You are

---

[12] Aussies are quite proud of their meat pies and there are special pie shops that are quite popular.

interrupting my personal phone conversation?' You want to walk straight out the door. Or what about being on hold for thirty minutes when calling a company to upgrade a service? All of this is very damaging to a brand and so easily avoidable.

So, make your customer service outstanding; it will be worth way more than you could ever imagine.

Facilitate interaction and build a community

Customer interaction and engagement is a huge value-add for your clients. Create a place where you, your clients and prospects can interact with each other, ask questions and get information. This can be done at a very low cost by using social media for example (more about this topic later).

Treat your clients like VIPS

Make sure you make your clients feel special. You could, for example, establish a members' club or run special events such as informational evenings or networking events. Each of these adds value for your clients and creates another opportunity for you to share your brand.

Make a difference

Finally, let's talk about one of our favourite topics: **contribution**. What has contribution got to do with branding? **A generous brand that is making a difference in the community is much more desirable than one that is not.** Just think for a second... If you go into a supermarket to buy a bottle of water and there are two different bottles next to each other for the exact same price, but one is contributing ten cents to a charity and the other one is not, which one would you grab? Exactly! Most people would go for the one supporting a good cause (given that price and quality are exactly the same).

Why not incorporate 'giving' into your business and make it a part of your brand. Support a great cause and get people to join you in an effort to make a difference. Good stuff!

A memorable brand is one that is different, stands out from the pack and takes a stance. Again, do not try to please everyone and market to all and sundry! By building a brand that stands out or differentiates itself from all the other competitors, you will attract a certain kind of person that will prefer to buy from you rather than from someone else because of what you represent.

"Matt, you need to pick your style; you can't just swap and change. One day you are a hippie, the next you are a nerd, and then you are an advertising dude. How are your girls ever going to know who you are and what you stand for? It's too confusing. Well, maybe you are just a bit confused and it's reflecting in your style."

"I know, mate. I've just been trying different styles lately to see what suits me best and also goes well with my lifestyle goals. What if I suddenly decide to change my style because I've outgrown being a hippie, or just because I've changed as a person and the hip advertising dude look doesn't suit me anymore?" Matt frowned.

"No problem, mate. You are not married to your style and you can certainly change it as you like." Fabio drew a long slow breath then continued. "It is absolutely normal that things can change; same goes for your personal brand. But there is one more thing you need to know, Matt...

"... Girls are like birds, beautiful birds of course. Look after one, treat her right, and before you know it you'll have a whole flock keeping their eyes on you. Even if you're with one that you know is not right, you want her telling her friends how good you are and spreading the word of 'Matt, the most generous and fabulous guy ever.' So, no matter what you're doing and who you're with, you should always do your best and deliver more than your lady expects."

This is a good time to look at your **Unique Selling Proposition** (USP). Your USP is everything that makes you stand out from your competitors.

What makes you different from the others? What makes your products or services unique? And why would someone buy from you rather than your competitors?

Your USP is not necessarily your tagline, but it will be the foundation from which you will determine a short, snappy and memorable tagline.

We are sure you remember these famous taglines:

Avis Rent a Car: *We try harder*

Apple Macintosh: *Think different*

Hallmark: *When you care enough to send the very best*

Kellogg's Rice Bubbles: *Snap! Crackle! Pop!*

(The last two were both created in the 1930s and are still going strong!)

A great way to think about your USP is to think about which aspects of your services your clients value more than anything. What would make them choose working with you over your competitors?

If you are a chiropractor, what about offering fresh fruit and juice in the waiting area? Or checking in a few days after a client's visit to make sure they are feeling great? Imagine if your GP called you after a visit to make sure you are feeling better. You would love her and would certainly talk about her amazing customer service to your family and friends. If you are a plumber, you could call your customers on the day and let them know that you will be on time or ten minutes early so that the client can make sure she is not in the shower when you get there! Now, that's service.

In summary, you want a brand that is worth falling in love with. The fastest way to do this is to live, breathe and share your vision and brand values. If you have got a brand worth following, you will create raving fans or brand ambassadors that will spread the love for you.

It's your turn to take action

1. Develop your brand: Have a think about what you want your brand to stand for and how you want it to be perceived, and then develop ideas about how you can achieve this.
2. Now let's define your USP. It's an invaluable exercise that will help you market your business more effectively. Write down why people should buy from you rather than your competitors—what makes you unique. Write down everything that comes to mind; this is no time to be humble! Ask some of your clients and prospects too; you'll get some valuable insights.

6

Building relationships

Not just a one night stand!

"The quality of your life is the quality of your relationships."

~ ANTHONY ROBBINS

FRIDAY AFTERNOON AS WORK WAS WINDING down, Matt grabbed two beers out of the fridge and walked over to Fabio's office. "Corona[13], Fabio?"

"Let's go down to the pub, mate. I need to get out of here. I've been in the office since six in the morning!

---

[13] Aussies generally prefer to drink Mexican beer (Coronas) and pay twice the price, rather than their own internationally famous beer, while Euros drink Fosters (Australia's most famous beer) and pay twice the price in Europe. Most Aussies have never even had a Fosters

Plus we can put into practice some of the stuff I taught you right away; I think you are ready."

"I can't wait. I'm so ready!" Matt had settled for a hip Euro-style look, his short hair a bit longer at the back, tight jeans with a black belt and funky sneakers.

"We'll see!" Fabio smiled.

They found a table in the beer garden, and as Fabio went to the bar to grab some beers, Matt saw a table with four cute girls talking in a foreign language. They must be tourists visiting Sydney, he thought. Perfect for testing my new branding. The good thing with foreigners is they are usually up for something short-lived as they're just passing through, so no 'baggage' except for their backpack. Perfect to practice what Fabio has taught me. With the inflated confidence of having his own personal Cupid just over at the bar, Matt made a move for the tourists and zeroed in on a gorgeous brunette.

"Excuse me. I really like your style. Can I get your number? Maybe we could go for a drink sometime?" Matt asked very politely and confidently. The girl looked stunned by Matt's surprise attack. Matt thought this girl was a total spunk[14]. Her brown mane looked even more gorgeous in the afternoon sun. She smiled apologetically and, obviously sorry for Matt's plump approach, told him she had a boyfriend and turned back to her friends, continuing as if nothing had happened. With his head down and tail between his legs, Matt walked back to his table.

"What are you doing, mate?" Fabio seemed annoyed. "This is not about getting laid by some poor

---

[14] A spunk is a good-looking person.

tourist! We are after some more sustainable strategies here! I'm glad you are finally ready for the most important concept; you obviously need it!" Fabio slammed two beer bottles onto the table.

"That didn't go down very well..." Matt looked like a kid found trying to steal a lolly from the lolly jar.

"Are you surprised? I hope not! I heard what you asked her. You can't just walk up to somebody and sound like you're asking them to jump into bed with you. It doesn't happen in personal or business relationships. You first need to build some sort of relationship before you can ask for the 'sale.'"

"I was just giving it a go. What if I don't have time to beat around the bush[15]?"

"Then you might as well just close your business!" Fabio's eyes narrowed. "You wanna know the secrets to getting lots of action?"

"Yes, please," said Matt with a slightly desperate tone.

"There is only one secret: You must focus on building relationships rather than making a 'sale.' That's it!"

"That's it? Sounds pretty easy... but then again, you always manage to make the most complicated things sound easy. Okay. Tell me more." Matt moved his chair closer to the table to not miss a word. He seemed to have already forgotten about his failed attempt with the brunette and was ready to move on.

---

[15] 'Beating around the bush' has got nothing to do with gardening or Brazilian waxing; it means 'dancing around the issue and not getting to the point'.

"Okay. Instead of walking over to a table of girls and asking for their phone numbers, you take it a bit slower and lead the girl you are interested in (your 'ideal client') through a series of little "yeses" in the lead up to the big "yes". The most important thing is that you make the first few steps low risk so that it is not scary for her to say "yes". You could maybe give her a little smile, flirt a little, say hello, so she becomes familiar with you and knows you won't bite... and then you buy her a drink... then you ask her if she'd like to go for coffee or breakfast... then you ask her for her number... then you take her for a walk... then you invite her for dinner... You get the picture?"

"I think I know what you mean. Instead of focusing on getting some action, I first need to do a bit of pre-work, take her for a walk on the beach, have dinner, maybe a little kiss, go to the movies..." Matt's face lit up with hope. "I'm keen for something longer term anyway, so this approach is much more sustainable!"

"You got it! That's exactly it! Take one step at a time and build trust. Let's get out of here and put this into practice at the Santorini Bar. It's obvious the brunette and her friends are not interested anyway."

You are now ready for one of the most important marketing lessons for small businesses. It will serve as the foundation for all of the marketing strategies to come: *relationship-based* or *trust-based marketing*[16].

The truth is that most marketing activities miss a huge portion of potential clients. When you hand out flyers at a networking event, for example, or run an advertisement in a paper or magazine, less than 5% of the people who receive the flyer or see the ad will be ready to buy from you right away. For the other 95%[17], it might not be the right time to buy your services or products.

But here is the distinction: they might be ready or wanting what you've got in a few days, months or even years. The dilemma is that because they are exposed to so many marketing messages every day, when they do want your products or services, they probably won't remember your flyer or advertisement. So, in order for you to stay in the front of potential clients' minds, you need to somehow keep in touch so that when they are ready to buy, they will remember you and choose you over any competitor.

---

[16] In his best-selling book *Permission Marketing*, Seth Godin talks about the concept of building relationships and its importance.

[17] These are approximate figures only, and the percentages change depending on how targeted your campaign and how effective your piece of marketing is.

So, how do you keep in touch?

The first thing you need to do is get them into your 'community.' You could invite them to be in your database to receive your mail-outs, get them to join your social media community and/or invite them to subscribe to your podcast or blog. The more touch points you have with your prospects and the higher the quality of them, the better. A little word of warning here: Make sure you do not spam prospects with constant sales emails and messages or they will leave your community in no time. You need to give them a good reason for being in your community and make them want to stay.

So, think about how you can create win-win situations to grow your database. In exchange for prospects giving you their details, at least their name and email address (Please do not send them stuff without their consent!), you have to offer something of highly perceived value that, most importantly, does not involve your time. Remember, your marketing systems are supposed to create more time for you rather than take it away! So think about what could be something of value to your ideal client, something you only have to create once but can give away hundreds of times without involving your time. It could be a free eBook or a book with 'How to' tips and tricks, a CD, a guide, a report, an online video or a DVD or even free shipping on their first order or special deals only available to your contacts.

You can set up a Database Management System[18] to collect your prospects details online in exchange for your free gift without you having to lift a finger. You could be watching your favourite re-run of *Dancing with the Stars* while your system is building your business for you. Remember, the more irresistible your offer is to your target market the better.

Once you have your prospective clients in your database (and they have their free gift), you can then stay in touch with them (with their permission) by sending a monthly, fortnightly or weekly email with some valuable information. Again, please make sure you do not just sell blatantly or they will leave.

The good news is that all of this can be systemised and automated so that your systems are pretty much building relationships for you.

In our own businesses (and our clients' businesses), we've implemented systems that help us automate our marketing efforts and send out email tips to people who have requested them. We create the system once and set it on autopilot. The emails will go out thousands of times over while we are focusing on other more important things such as going on a holiday or taking the kids to the zoo. The system pretty much does the marketing for us; it's

---

[18] A database management system, or customer relationship system (CRM) as it is also called, is a piece of software that helps you manage your database effectively. More about that later.

like our best employee that always does a perfect job.

Once our prospects are ready to take the next step, they give us a call and most of them are usually ready to get going because the system has pre-positioned them, built trust and created familiarity. So, even when we are overseas, our systems are working for us. While working and travelling through Europe for three months, our marketing systems helped us grow our business while we were drinking French wine and eating Swiss cheese and chocolate[19].

The purpose of staying in touch with and in front of potential clients is to build trust and familiarity by constantly adding value.

If you go to **www.basicbananas.com**, you will see our opt in form on the top right of every website page. Put your name and email address into the form and you will receive our free, valuable marketing resources and see how we do it. We make sure we provide a lot of value and look after our contacts. This is important! Be generous and keep giving, and you'll be taken care of.

Our clients absolutely love having systems in place. Let's look at some more practical examples.

---

[19] Well, besides eating too much Swiss chocolate, we were also working a couple of hours a day.

Example 1: Valuable gift

Kieron[20], an electrician, had been spending a lot of money on ads in the local newspaper and on letterbox drops, and he also went networking. But he still did not have enough clients to keep him busy. So, the first thing we did was look at how he managed to build relationships and create trust with his prospects. As with most businesses, Kieron did not focus on building relationships at all. He had been in business for eleven years and didn't even have a database. What a bummer. Imagine if he had built his database over eleven years with say 5,000 people in it. (That's less than 500 new contacts a year). He would never run out of business if he stayed in touch with them on a regular basis by giving them some valuable tips and information. There would always be somebody who knows somebody who needs an electrician. And in his potential customers' eyes, Kieron would increase his chances of being the right person if he had been generously looking after his database.

So, in order to get people's interest in Kieron's services, we created a small guide on how to save money on your electricity bill, knowing that most people would be happy to get some tips on how to save a few dollars. Kieron then put his offer for the

---

[20] The names in all examples have been changed due to privacy reasons.

free guide onto his website, his brochures and even in his ads. It looked something like this:

> Email info@example.com to receive your free guide, *10 tips to save 10% on your electricity.*

So, instead of saying, 'Give me money, buy my stuff' (in a subtle way), he offered something of value in return for people's contact details. Within six months of changing his strategy, he had over 600 people in his database receiving monthly valuable tips on how to save money, best energy rates, newest innovations and so on—and everything was set up automatically. So, while he was out working or playing with his kids, he was growing his business on autopilot!

This model has completely revolutionised Kieron's business and rather than chasing client after client, he now has a constant flow of clients coming to him. Even though not all 600 people have used his services, Kieron is building relationships with them, and once they are in need of an electrician (or know somebody who is), they will certainly remember Kieron who has been so kind to provide them with valuable information. He can also use this list of contacts to send something cool in the mail (more about that in *Chapter 11 Lumpy Mail*).

We have successfully used this strategy with a number of our clients.

Another effective method of building relationships with prospective clients is through giving away samples of your products. In his book *Influence: The Psychology of Persuasion*, Dr. Robert Cialdini talks about the Law of Reciprocity and how people have a need to reciprocate a gift even if they did not want it in the first place. This feeling to have to reciprocate is a result of society's conditioning.

An example is when a business gives away a free sample of something rather than trying to get you to buy straight away. A 'give-away' is basically a sample of the bigger picture that leaves the client wanting even more. We experienced a classic example of this strategy being used really well by a tiny bakery in Santiago de Compostela, a city in the north of Spain.

Example 2: Free product sample

This tiny retail bakery was located in a narrow but busy cobblestone street, next to a few other bakeries competing for customers. Two ladies dressed in traditional Spanish clothes stood in front of the shop with a large silver plate, offering their home-style almond cookies to the passers-by (mostly tourists visiting the famous pilgrimage city). How could we not stop and try a sampling when a lovely lady with such a warm smile was pretty much shoving a plate of sweets in front of us? And once we tried the cookies, the ladies invited us into the bakery to try another local treat. The owners knew that once the customers are in the shop, they most likely will buy something; how could they not? Their strategy to capture the attention of passers-by worked extremely well because, as you would guess, we purchased some lovely almond cookies and other local treats!

The law of reciprocity applied to this transaction because once we tried the free sample we felt a little oliged to buy something.

It's your turn to take action

1. Create something of value for your prospects, maybe a free guide, weekly tips, recipes for success, product reviews, video, audio or a free trial. Be creative and think about what would be valuable for your clients.

2. Set up a Database Management System or Customer Relationship Management Systems (if you do not have one already). You need somewhere to store your clients' and prospective clients' names, addresses, email addresses, hone numbers, what it is they are interested in and any other details that may be beneficial[21].

---

[21] When you collect details through your website, the less information you ask for, the more people will generally opt in. So your conversion rate goes up if you only ask for an email address, but the quality of your leads goes down.

There are many different programs out there that are great for this and also for automating your communications with your database contacts, for example, sending emails out at pre-determined intervals. There are many different programs out there that are great for this and also for automating your communications with your database contacts, for example, sending emails out at pre-determined intervals.

If you go to our website **basicbananas.com** you will find a link to the software we are using—Ontraport. Otherwise MailChimp, Constant Contact or Aweber work well too.

3. Once your database is set up, you need to start recording details of every prospective, existing and past customer. Keep in touch with your contacts by, for example, sending a monthly newsletter or fortnightly tips (with their permission). Think about what is something you can give away that will make your prospects want more. The most important thing is that you look after your database and do not burn them out by flogging your stuff in every email.

4. Got to **www.basicbananas.com** and opt in to see how we have set up our system. We use a combination of short video and email tips to keep it interesting. Study how we have set this up because a lot of testing and measuring has gone into creating our systems. You are welcome to copy anything we do to help you succeed.

PART 2

Kick-Butt Marketing Strategies to Attract More Clients and Grow Your Business

How to get the girls... whoops... prospects begging for more.

7

Networking

Working the field

"It's not what you know but who you know that makes the difference."

~ UNKNOWN

"MATT!" FABIO YELLED ACROSS THE CORRIDOR TO where Matt was standing swearing at the photocopier. "I've got some great news for you!"

"Shhhh, not so loud Fabio... I don't want the entire ad agency to know about this stuff." Matt grabbed Fabio's arm and pulled him into a meeting room, closing the door behind them.

"Come on, dude. Half the agency already knows about it anyway!" Fabio's grin was bigger than a volcanic crack.

"Oh no," Matt groaned. "You couldn't keep your mouth shut, could you?... Oh well, half the agency is better than the whole, I suppose. But, please, from now on," Matt was turning red, "let's keep this under wraps, okay?"

"No worries[22]. I'll do my best. Anyway, I saw on Facebook that there is a big singles party on at the Cat Club this Saturday, and I think you should go and apply your new strategies! One of my friends is organising it and I can get you a free ticket." The well-connected Fabio loved showing off his connections.

"Are you coming with me?" Matt was feeling a bit out of his comfort zone and not so sure about going to a singles party; he had never been to one before.

"No, mate. I'd like to, and I'm sure I'd still have a high score. But I don't think my wifey would be too happy about it. You'll be fine! Singles parties are fun, and you can tell me all about it on Monday."

"Hmmm. Ok, I'll go. Surely I'll be able to meet a girl at a singles party. There'll be a lot of desperate people there—so I'll fit right in then!" Matt attempted a touch of humour as he relaxed a bit more.

The following Monday morning, Matt was typing away at his desk when Fabio stopped by and asked him about how the singles party went.

"Let's not talk about it." Matt didn't even look up from his computer. Fabio figured Matt either had Monday-itis or he didn't have a good weekend... He guessed it was the latter.

---

[22] No worries: It means there's nothing to worry about, it's okay. It reflects Aussie national stoicism.

"Doesn't sound very promising. We might have to add some more strategies to increase your success rate." Fabio put his tanned hand onto Matt's shoulder. "Didn't you meet even one nice girl?"

"Yes, lots of nice girls... but none were interested. I started to wonder whether I had bad breath or something, but I didn't. Every time I spoke to a nice girl, it took her about 3 ½ minutes to decide that she needed to go to the toilet or get another drink—one even pretended to get a phone call. How ridiculous is that?" Matt was still typing furiously as if to punish his keyboard for his bad luck... or was it bad skills?

"Tell me exactly what you did in those 3 ½ minutes." Fabio looked like a love guru out of a bad Hollywood movie with his funky Hawaiian shirt and dark, shoulder-length hair flowing loose today.

"I didn't do anything. I just spoke about what I do for work, my favourite hobbies, my work promotions, etcetera. My most impressive stuff that should impress the pants off a girl!"

"Oh man, you fell into the 'I am so important and I can't stop talking about myself' trap." Fabio shook his head. "I should have warned you about this, but to be honest, I didn't think you were that kind of guy."

"That kind of guy? What the heck do you mean?" Matt finally stopped typing and looked up.

"All right, I'll give you the short version because I'm about to run into a meeting. The biggest mistake people make, and trust me you are not alone, is that they just talk about themselves all the time and never listen. Very unattractive. Whenever you meet a prospective girl, you must show curiosity, ask questions and listen, rather than talk about yourself.

Unless you are the Pope or Richard Branson, people don't want to hear every detail about you and your life on your first encounter. As you know, and have proven yourself, most people love talking about themselves; so listening is one of the greatest gifts you can give them. At the end of the one-way conversation they will say, 'That was such a great conversation, even though it was one-sided.' Give it a go and you will see for yourself."

"Kinda makes sense, Fabio. Maybe I need to go to another singles party so I can put that into practice." Matt still looked a bit grumpy but he felt a bit better knowing that most people would make that same mistake.

"You know what? The best thing you can do is put it into practice with your advertising clients. Next time you pick up the phone or have a meeting, just let them speak. They will love you for it. That's all I do with my clients and they love me—no rocket-science there." Fabio was as confident as always.

Networking can be one of the most effective marketing strategies for small business owners, if done right. It also works especially well for start-up businesses that are just getting out there and testing the grounds. We have worked with a lot of start-ups that have kick-started their business by going to networking events to connect with other business owners and have attracted their very first clients this way.

If you are a solopreneur, networking not only helps you grow your business, but you also get to hang out with like-minded people, connect and share your experiences.

Networking is like planting seeds. Every time you go to a networking event, you are planting seeds. What most business owners forget, though, is that seeds need to be nurtured, watered and looked after before you can reap the fruits. You usually can't plant seeds and hope to have fruits straight away.

For your networking efforts to be effective and pay off, you need to look after the contacts you make. Stay in touch with some of the people you meet and focus on building relationships rather than hoping for a quick sale. So many people go networking because they are hoping to sell something rather than hoping to find good connections to buy from. Imagine being in a room full of fifty people whose only reason for being there is to sell something! Good luck! The quality of your relationships has a huge impact on your business success.

So, how do you cultivate your contacts?
There are many ways to look after your contacts. You could send someone a gift related to their particular interests; for example, an article on a hobby or interest they have, a book they might find

interesting or a relevant business article. When somebody gives you their business card and you start chatting to them about golf or fast cars or business ideas—whatever it is—make a little note on the back of their card so you remember their interests. A little extra tip for you: writing down details about somebody you meet is smart as you are most likely not going to remember who said what. Just use their business cards to write a little note about them. Don't do it in front of them, maybe, so you do not look like you are defacing their business card.

If you go to networking events hoping to sell something, you need to change your mindset and start thinking about how you can provide value. It will make a massive difference in your business and how people perceive you in the business world. You will naturally attract more prospects.

Make sure you do not go around the room asking everybody the same questions. It doesn't always have to be a business-related conversation either. People are so much more than their business, and talking about a common interest, no matter what the topic is, can create a strong sense of connection. Sincere compliments are good too. For example, 'I really like your necklace.' It has to be completely authentic though. Don't walk up to a guy with the messiest hair and ask him where he gets his hair cut, unless you really do like his hairstyle, of course.

A great post-networking strategy is to set up 'Coffee Chats'—an individual catch-up for a coffee. When you meet interesting people you could have great synergies with and are potential strategic alliance partners, or maybe you would just like to learn more about them and their business, suggest meeting up for a Coffee Chat. This can even be a virtual coffee, if you would like to save time or if distance is an issue. Just set up a phone chat. Of course, a lot of people still do prefer face-to-face meetings. [A health expert would probably advise that instead of drinking five coffees a day because of Coffee Chats, why not order a tea or fresh juice to switch it up a bit? A 'tea chat.'

This is what you do not do at the meeting: Talk about yourself for an hour! Yes, we know; it has happened to all of us. We have had this painful experience of sitting opposite someone who just would not stop talking about themselves. So, please avoid being that type of person and show a genuine curiosity in others. Ask about their business and how you could support them. If you are not interested in their business or them, then just don't suggest a Coffee Chat. The catch up is not there for you to flog your stuff and waste someone's time. That's actually pretty rude. As Fabio taught Matt above... *Zip it!* Stop talking about yourself and your business; you will turn people off like a sweaty guy sitting on your beach towel in his sluggos[23].

Instead of focusing on yourself and how good you are, focus on the business owners you meet. Keep the focus of the conversation on them. People love being heard, so be attentive and listen. They will love you for that. Your turn to speak will come, and when it does, be curious and ask them questions. Apologies for being repetitive about this one; it's just so crucial to you and your business's success.

How often do you meet people that just do not stop talking about themselves? You find yourself thinking of a way to get out of the conversation or hope for a friend to come over and rescue you. Kurt, whose business was selling phones, was the worst networker you could imagine! All he would do is walk up to people (usually trying to chase every single person in the room), talk about his business, and as soon as he realised that the guy or girl wasn't interested in buying his stuff, he would bugger[24] off and talk to the next person. You know how many

---

[23] Sluggos, also known as 'Budgie Smugglers': A swim brief for men such as those worn in competitive swimming and diving. There were mixed reviews of the Australian Prime Minister, Tony Abbot's, wearing sluggos in a public surf race. Some said we don't need to know what polis are packing into their sluggos but rather what words are coming out of their mouth.

[24] British slang that means to leave someone alone; to go away. The real roots of the meaning are too rude to put here!

phones he sold? That's right, none. Did he build any relationships for future business? No. Could somebody have been interested or known someone who could be? Yes, but he missed out on all of that by not showing any interest in anybody but himself (Well, he actually sold the biggest travel phones ever seen that must have been from the last century. So, we're not sure if anyone would have really wanted them anyway).

Another great networking tip is to keep an eye out for newbies and make them feel comfortable. Most people get pretty nervous when going to a brand new networking event and might feel a little bit lost and alone. You can help them feel comfortable by introducing them to others and welcoming them into your group of people if they are standing alone. Why? Because you are a good girl or guy and you care.

When you meet people, you could ask them whether they would be interested in receiving your free monthly tips. Most people will say 'yes' if they see the value in receiving your emails. Then sit back and let your systems build relationships for you. Okay, yes, human contact is even better but you've only got limited hours in your days. Sometimes you just can't meet everyone without compromising your ideal lifestyle (Remember the start of the book!). You might want to save a few hours to go to the beach, hang out with friends or play with your dog.

However, to do this, you must have systems working for you.

> ### It's your turn to take action
>
> As discussed earlier, having a database of prospects is what makes your business so valuable, so you should always be on the look-out for ways to grow your database, and networking is one such way.
>
> Go to at least one networking event per month. If you really want to ramp your business up, we suggest you go to two networking events a week for the next 90 days. Let's call it a '90-Day Networking Challenge,' and you will see your business fly.

Getting your website online

Welcome to the cyber world!

"The internet is becoming the town square for the global village of tomorrow."

~ BILL GATES

A WEEK LATER, MATT WENT TO ANOTHER SINGLES party, and guess what? He applied all the principles Fabio had taught him and the results blew his mind; he went home with the phone numbers of five interested girls! One of them had really caught Matt's attention, a gorgeous blonde with long, silky hair, a beautiful, young, healthy complexion and blue eyes that made Matt's head spin—Anna McKenzie.

Although Matt could not stop thinking about Anna, no real progress had been made that night with her, and he still cheekily loved to check out what else was on the market. What better and safer way than to check online; there were so many websites for him to check out other girls. (No, not porn sites, but partner searching and social media sites).

A couple of days later while Matt was flicking through the single ladies on a dating site, he thought of Anna for the millionth time and decided (finally) to 'google' her name to see what he could find online about her. Her profile on LinkedIn came up straight away. Then he got onto Facebook to see what she was interested in, what her friends were saying about her and what they were saying to each other. He checked her pictures and any other information he could find. Luckily for him, she didn't have any privacy settings set up so he had full access to her pictures and information. (Though he did think that once they were together, he would definitely show her how to amend her privacy settings!)

Nowadays, researching about someone is so easy to do. You don't have to get face to face with anyone or ask them questions that could be uncomfortable or seem intrusive. You can just go online. So, Matt learned all about Anna from the comfort of his own home while in his Superman pyjamas, drinking a VB. He liked what he saw and was even more determined to meet up with her. He was just not sure what his plan of attack should be. So once again he thought about asking Relationship King Fabio for advice.

We regularly have small business owners ask us to recommend reliable providers of various services, so we decided to conduct a little experiment of our own. Between January, 2011 to July, 2011 every business owner who asked us to refer someone to them (web developers, graphic designers, printers or a variety of other business-related providers) they were given the details of two suppliers. So, when someone asked us if we knew a good web developer, we would give them the contact details of two great web developers. A week or two later, we would contact the business owner to find out if they used either of the providers we recommended, why they decided to use them, and what made them choose one provider over the other.

The results were interesting and clearly showed us that the two main reasons someone would choose one supplier over the other were:

- the supplier's manner (mostly over the phone) and genuine interest in the prospects and their needs; and
- the supplier's website.

This experiment gave us some awesome insights into the power of communicating with potential clients (Be polite and curious, people!) and that your website is the first place potential clients go to check you out.

The majority of people looking to choose a business will check you out online before buying from you. We are pretty sure that if you ask your clients, most of them will confirm that they checked you out online before deciding to work with you. So, it is up to you to maximise your online presence; your website is your shopfront.

We regularly have clients tell us that they have checked out not only our website but also our social media activity, and they read reviews online before making a decision to work with us. In most cases, our online presence and activities have attracted and converted clients for us without us lifting a finger.

Through the web, not only do potential clients have access to what people are saying about a business and what a business has to say about itself, but they also get to look at the competition. It is all available right at their fingertips. So you will be better placed if you maximise your presence online. The first thing a potential client will look at is your website. In this chapter we are focusing on your website. Further on, we will look at social media and some other innovative online strategies.

Why do you need a website?

Your website is not just a brochure. It is a lead generation tool and can work for you even when you are asleep or visiting the Taj Mahal in India. A 'lead' is anyone who enquires, is referred to you or opts in to your database. It is basically anyone you can follow up.

In Matt's case, a lead could be an interested look across a bar or a girl who 'Likes' his status on Facebook or becomes 'friends' with him on social media.

A website is also a fabulous credibility tool—a credibility statement—that proves yours is an established business. It is a place where your prospects can go to find out more information about you and decide whether you are the one to contact or not. Visitors can check your services and pricing and read testimonials. Customer reviews or testimonials are incredibly powerful and influence a potential buyer's decision to buy either from you or from another provider. If you do not have a website where prospects can access this information, then you most likely won't make it into their equation.

As mentioned earlier, the more your business is in front of your prospects, the more familiarity you will build. Do you know a business whose name you see popping up everywhere? As you become more and more familiar with the business, and if it has a great reputation, you will feel more inclined to do business with them when you are ready.

The good thing about a website is it allows people to find out more about you and your business in a non-threatening way from the comfort of their own home. (Aren't we a scared and comfort-loving bunch?) And we are yet to come across somebody who does not know how to 'google' a business name; even those who are not tech savvy can do it.

Your website will give you access to a whole planet of potential clients you might not have otherwise had access to. It opens up a whole new market.

And finally, nowadays (and more and more) people love buying online. It is convenient, fast and easy. You can buy almost anything online. If you chose to, you could never leave the house again and you would survive. Well, maybe you would have a lack of Vitamin D from missing out on sunlight, but everything else you need can be purchased online and delivered straight to your door... Actually, you could even buy Vitamin D tablets online.

One of the most important things that distinguish your business from your competitors is the content of your website. The website must look professional and be consistent with your overall branding.

Hopefully you are now convinced that you need a website (if you do not have one already). So, let's look at the different types of websites out there.

What kind of website do you need?

Your website should be a stepping stone that leads your visitors wherever you want them to go. The type of website you choose for your business will depend on your desired outcome.

Therefore, when choosing a website, first think about the purpose of your site:

- *What do you want it to do for you?*
- *Where do you want people to go?*
- *What do you want them to do?*

There is a wide range of different websites to choose from, depending on your desired outcome and your objectives for your site:

Brochure style credibility statement

This is just a nice website that informs people about you and your business, your products, your team and so on. Make sure you have an opt-in form/box to collect your prospects' details.

Long Sales Letter

This type of site is just one long page with the purpose of selling only one product or service. It usually has some kind of special offer and keeps asking the viewer to buy it NOW. The results show that long sales letters do work, even though we have hardly come across anybody who loves them. Our personal preference is to use a video rather than a long sales letter to sell a product or service.

Online Store or Ecommerce Site

This is an online shop where people can view your range and buy your products directly online. This site is very common and useful. The big brands have now jumped on board this trend as well, successfully selling their goods online in addition to having a store.

Landing Page

This is a one-page site where people can only do one thing. Usually that is to put their details into a form in return for some free stuff, registering for an event or buying something. Embedding a video on a landing page is a great way to promote a product or event or to encourage viewers to opt in. It can be a fabulous tool to grow your database. Your database would be like Matt's little black book full of girls' phone numbers (not that he has one). When you have a lot of interested contacts, you will never have a problem making a sale. A landing page can be much shorter than a long sales letter-type website. It might only include a video explaining what you want your visitor to do and a registration or 'Buy now' form.

Members Only Site

This type of site provides extra value for your clients because they can access resources and information 24/7 without having to contact you. They are a great tool to use as a bonus for your clients or as part of your services.

Internal Site

This is a site that is accessed only by your team members and improves productivity by providing a central location for them to get information or common documents.

Employee Training Site

This is another type of team members only site that is a central place that replaces the old ops manual and conveniently displays staff training videos, procedure manuals, to-do lists and so on. We love this one for our team members as it increases productivity and quality of work.

You can also choose a combination of any of the above. For example, if your primary purpose for having a website is to make sales online, the content of your homepage needs to get the viewer excited about your product and lead them in the direction they need to go in order to buy.

Most websites out there do not lead you anywhere; they often just state how fantastic the business, business owner or products are and expect people to search around on the site and work out for themselves what to do next or how to buy. But they won't!

If you want to increase your response rate online, before creating your site define a clear path that you would like your visitors to follow.

One of our clients, a website developer (!), doubled his leads within three weeks of working with us by simply adding an opt-in box to his website and changing the copy slightly. A significant increase in leads for him considering he had been in business for over ten years!

The stats are quite scary. It is believed that the average time a person will spend on a website before leaving again is less than seven seconds. And if you do not grab their attention straight away, they will get distracted by something else on the web, and you may lose a potential sale.

It gets worse though. They say less than 4% of people will ever return to a website! So, within that initial seven seconds that someone is on your site, you need to grab their attention with a clear and engaging headline, preferably stating the benefits of what you offer and who it is for, or by using engaging imagery. Your website should capture people's attention instantly like a flasher in a busy city street.

Your content then needs to lead the reader from the headline to the next step you want them to take. Like stepping stones, your website content should lead your ideal client from the first step to the next through your headline and engaging copywriting, all the way to opting in, buying your product or picking up the phone. If any one of the stepping stones is a slippery one—off topic, boring or a link to another website—then you will most likely lose the reader.

Most small business websites can increase response rates by shifting the focus of their content to be about the benefits of their product for prospects rather than about themselves, their qualifications, their team, how long they have been in business, the names of their dog and cat and their favourite movie.

The right ingredients for a killer website

By now you are probably getting the idea that there are a lot of variables for a website. It has to:

- be functional
- build your credibility
- create relationships
- grow your database
- talk to your ideal clients

Let's look at the different ingredients you need to make your website work well for you.

Ingredient 1: Write an attention grabbing headline

Write down at least 20 possible headlines and ask a few people for feedback. Then pick the best one. You might even change it along the way. Test and measure your results.

Ingredient 2: Don't make it all about you!

Make it all about THEM. Write content that is conversational and 'talking' to your prospects. Make sure you add the benefits of your product. Do not make your website too text-heavy. No one likes too much blah blah blah...

Ingredient 3: Highlight your benefits

Think about what your product/service's main benefits are for your clients, and make them clear on your home page. This will also help you engage the right people.

Ingredient 4: Have a Call to Action

Tell the viewer what to do next, for example, 'Enter your details now to receive your free report,' 'Call now for a free quote.' Tell your visitors exactly what you want them to do.

Ingredient 5: Put engaging stuff above the fold

Make sure your most important information is 'above the fold.' This refers to everything you can see on a webpage without having to scroll down. You do not want your visitors to have to scroll down to get to the essential parts.

Ingredient 6: Make your contact details clearly visible

Add your contact details (at least your phone number) to every page so that it is easy for your prospects to get in touch with you.

Ingredient 7: Add an opt-in box

If your website is attracting a lot of traffic and you don't have a way of collecting people's details to start building relationships, you are missing out on a lot of opportunities. To encourage prospective ideal clients (leads) to leave their details, create an irresistible offer for some 'Free Stuff' for which they will leave their details in your lead capture box. This will give you the opportunity to build a relationship with them by providing value and will show that you are generous and know your stuff.

This strategy is based on the concept of permission (or relationship) based marketing. As discussed earlier, you get the prospect to take action and ask for your free information. The better your offer is, the more you will get people opting in, and not just any people, but people who are interested in what you have. So, you end up with a long list of interested prospects that you can build a relationship with.

We have business owners in our programs who will never have a problem finding clients again because they have done a fantastic job of building and looking after (not spamming) their database. They are in a position where they can make a special offer from time to time with a series of emails that will start a buying frenzy. Remember, providing value is the secret ingredient that will make this work.

The cool thing is this can all be set up to happen automatically by email. You can be sipping a shangri-la and enjoying the sunset while your systems are busy marketing for you.

Ingredient 8: Collect testimonials and success stories

Ask your happy clients for feedback and permission to use it on your website. Also, ask them for a photo you could use with the testimonial or if they could say something on video when you next work with them... and Bob's your uncle ('and Bob's your uncle' is an Aussie saying meaning something along the lines of 'as easy as that').

Ingredient 9: Integrate your social media sites

Set up your Facebook, Instagram, Twitter, YouTube and LinkedIn pages, and add the icons to your website so that people can follow you on your social media pages. Integrating your social media tools shows the viewer that you are well-established and have a strong online presence that allows them to easily check you out. This builds more familiarity with you and your brand. Plus they can see that other people love your products or services, so you must be good!

Ingredient 10: Use great images that appeal to your market

The use of images on your website (and in your marketing materials) is important as your target market will identify themselves with the people in your pictures. So, make sure you find some images that talk to your prospects. Just make sure you are not breaching any copyright. There are many great websites where you can buy royalty-free images such as iStockphoto, Bigstock and Getty Images.

Adding a Frequently Asked Questions (FAQ) page is an optional extra. A FAQ page can save you time by answering questions commonly asked by prospects, and if done right it will help you sell your stuff. The beauty about this is that you get to choose your questions and answers. Think of questions and answers that position you as the best choice to buy from.

Eliminate other providers by highlighting your benefits. For example, if you have 20 years of experience and a guarantee, you could add a question like:

Q: How do I know I'm getting good quality?

And answer it with something like:

A: Whether you buy from us or any other provider of <insert your product or service>, make sure your provider has a minimum of 20 years of experience and check the guarantee they promise. We provide a full money back guarantee.

It looks like a conversation between a prospect and the provider, but you are in control. Pretty nifty idea, hey? So, make a list of your most frequently asked questions and write answers that position you as the logical solution. Think of the benefits of your product or service and highlight these with some of your questions and answers.

Google Analytics

As with all marketing strategies, you really need to measure your results so you can continue to improve or drop a strategy if it's not producing a positive return.

Google Analytics is a fabulous free tool that helps you measure your website's success. It tells you interesting stuff like how many people visit your site, where they came from, which pages people viewed, how long they stayed on your site and plenty of other valuable information.

Get it installed on your website and start tracking how many people are visiting your site weekly. It will assist you to track how effective your marketing efforts are.

It is easy to install yourself. Just search for 'Google Analytics' in Google. Otherwise, ask your website developer and it will be up and running in a matter of minutes.

It's your turn to take action

1. Decide on the purpose and objectives of your website.
2. Define the path you want your website visitors to follow.
3. Create a clear and engaging headline to capture their attention.
4. Write conversational copy focusing on the benefits to your prospects.
5. Have a clear Call to Action.
6. Put engaging content above the fold.
7. Make your contact details clearly visible.
8. Add an opt-in form to collect details.
9. Collect testimonials and success stories.
10. Connect your website with social media sites.
11. Include images that relate to the market.
12. Test and measure using Google Analytics.
13. Have FUN!

9

Social media

Socialising online

"By giving people the power to share, we're making the world more transparent."

~ MARK ZUCKERBERG, FOUNDER OF FACEBOOK

MATT COULDN'T TAKE HIS MIND OFF ANNA, AND HIS WORK started to slack off a little. He was even thinking about chucking a sickie[25] just because he didn't feel motivated at work. Most days he seemed a bit distracted, and his team members often caught him on Facebook, switching the screen immediately when

---

[25] 'Chucking a sickie' means taking a day off work even though you are perfectly healthy. If chucking a sickie was an Olympic sport, Australia would probably win the gold medal. Aussies love chucking a sickie just because the surf is good or they had a big night out

somebody walked past. He was checking out Anna's Facebook profile, watching her every move. He also found her on Twitter, and on LinkedIn he found out that she was a fashion designer working for a small label in Sydney. He also saw that she'd had lots of role changes in the past, which made him wonder about her commitment level to something. Maybe she was a bit of a flake[26]. But then again, she was Gen Y.

Tuesday morning, just before lunch, Fabio walked into Matt's office and interrupted him wasting time on Facebook.

"Mate, you better not spend too much time on social media sites at work. The big boss doesn't like it, and I hear you've been slacking off a bit!" Fabio sat on Matt's desk. "What's been going on? Any progress with that Anna girl you met at the singles party? You've been very quiet."

"All good. Just been busy and, yeah, probably wasting a bit of time stalking Anna." Matt sounded tired. "I must admit I haven't been very productive lately."

"Just make sure the big boss doesn't catch you mucking around[27] all day. You can do your stalking after work." Fabio was like a dad telling his kid to get his homework done before the mum comes home.

"You're right, 'Dad,' I better pick up my game. While you are here, do you have some more tips for me?" Matt quizzed Fabio. "I'm not making fast progress." As he looked at Fabio's dark brown eyes,

---

[26] A 'flake' is someone who pulls out of things at the last minute and doesn't follow through.
[27] 'Mucking around': act a goat, act a fool, play up.

Matt briefly wondered how old Fabio could be, guessing him to be over 45, but with the charisma of a 30-year-old rock star.

Fabio pulled the sleeves of his black Italian designer shirt up, ready to get into action. "Yes, I do have some more stuff for you. Talking about social media, do you think your Anna girl is looking you up on those social media sites as well? Even if she is only slightly interested, she would be for sure, right? That's what we do nowadays. It's never been so easy to research somebody. You've obviously been doing it 24/7."

Matt seemed very happy to hear that until Fabio continued...

"And she'd be thinking Wow, what a larrikin[28], he parties and drinks a lot, with all your party pictures on your Facebook profile. I think they paint the wrong picture of you. Not exactly a very good first, well second, impression. You better take down those pictures where you look a bit cross-eyed and sitting on random car bonnets."

Matt slumped and turned as red as a German tourist after a day on the beach. "Oh no! I totally didn't think about that. It didn't even cross my mind that she might be checking me out too. I was so consumed by researching her that..." He swung his seat around, clicked on Facebook and started looking through his pictures. "Oh, crap. This is no good!"

"You better lift your profile, mate! Remember when we discussed your personal brand? This is all part of it. Put some nice pictures up of you and your

---

[28] A 'larrikin' is a wild, mischievous and carefree person, or in Matt's case a party animal

mate's dog. Girls like that kind of fluff!" And in a girl's voice he added "Ahh, isn't he so cute with his puppy dog?"

"Good idea, Fabio! I'm gonna also upload some shots of me spending time with my family, so I look like a good guy. Well, I am a good guy, but you're right. I'm not showing that on Facebook! Oh, and maybe I'll Photoshop myself into a picture with Bono from U2." Matt got excited again.

"I wouldn't fake stuff, Matt! Well, the puppy dog story is ok; it's not really faking. Oh, and it helps when people are saying nice stuff about you. It's what you know as 'testimonials' in marketing terms. OK. Gotta go. Some of us have work to do!" With that, Fabio got up and walked out.

"Thanks, mate!" Matt shouted after Fabio as he hit the delete button on an image of himself pulling his pants down.

If you have not embraced social media for your business yet, it's time to get onto it! Do not put it off any longer. It's not something that will go away the longer you wait.

Social media is a fabulous marketing tool, not only to promote your business but also to build trust and relationships with prospects, giving you access to a huge online audience. It has never been so easy to sell your products or services globally. You are no longer limited just to your local market—the whole world is at your fingertips. Social media is a new way to get brand awareness versus spending lots of money on advertisements, radio ads, TV ads and billboards—money a small business usually doesn't have.

Social media is also called 'social networking' because that is exactly what it is—an online networking opportunity. You get to meet and connect with people worldwide from the comfort of your own home while sitting in your trackies. It does of course not substitute for 'face to face' networking. Human contact is still important, even in the 21st century! Even though some people promise you can build your whole empire while sitting in your undies—and you can—combining online and offline strategies will definitely accelerate your success. We have proven that over and over again with our clients.

A crucial concept to make social media work for you is to **add value *versus* sell**. If you only take away one thing from this chapter, this is what it should be: **Provide as much value as possible whenever you can, and your business will grow, guaranteed.**

Instead of using your social media to blatantly sell (and yes, a few people unfortunately do not get this and all they post or tweet are mini sales pitches that cause people to unsubscribe from their social media networks), you must provide **good content**.

This way people will love being on your networks and tell their friends about you too. By being in your network, they will become more familiar with your brand and build trust, which naturally leads to sales.

Another principle that works pretty much across all social media tools is to **engage your audience** and ask for interaction, getting people to participate in discussions. The more you interact and your prospects engage with you and each other, the better. It will attract more people and expand your network quickly.

Social media is also a fantastic tool to conduct research on businesses and people. Just like 'googling' a business to find your website, a lot of prospects will be looking you up on social media and checking what others are saying about you before deciding to work with you.

To give an example, Jordan, a web designer, called us up out of the blue one day to sign up to one of our marketing programs. When we asked him how he found out about us, he said a friend who saw us speak at an event recommended us. So, he jumped onto Facebook and LinkedIn, watched a few videos on YouTube and opted in through our website. He had been in our database for over three months, receiving our fortnightly marketing tips without us lifting a finger. Our systems built a relationship and trust with him to the point where he was ready to buy.

That is what we want your marketing systems to do for you, so you can spend your time doing what you love or what you are most effective at. And let's be honest, a lot of small business owners do not love marketing. But you have to do marketing if you want to attract clients and grow your business. Either you can outsource it or bite the bullet and get a mentor, or take some courses and just do it. Our recommendation is to learn how to be in charge of your marketing as it is a great skill to have.

The big four social media players we will look at are **Facebook, Twitter, LinkedIn** and **YouTube**. They each have their own strengths and weaknesses.

We will look at them individually so you can determine which ones you would like to use for your own business—a combination of a few is good. Having said that, it is better to focus on one or two tools and do them really well, rather than focus on seven and do a semi-decent job. The good news is that there are a few applications that link all your accounts with each other so you can leverage your time and efforts. Plus, once you have a great strategy in place, you can get somebody else to manage it for you, as long as you keep an eye on it. A word of warning here; there are quite a few so-called 'social media experts' out there that happily take your money without delivering the results they promise or really knowing what they are doing. It is your brand after all, and you know best how you want to be perceived, your tone of voice and so on.

Facebook

Facebook is one of our personal favourites as it works really well for a lot of small business owners, and Mark Zuckerberg, the founder, and his team keep developing fabulous additions to make it one of the best social media tools.

Facebook has a personal and business side to it. It is really important to distinguish between the two. Business fan pages are there for commercial use, whereas your personal profile is not supposed to be used for business. Facebook can delete your account if they find your personal page being used commercially.

Facebook allows you to build a strong community around your business and create raving fans that will spread the word for you. As mentioned earlier, the better the content that you are sharing on Facebook, the more fans you will attract and your community will grow. If you keep trying to sell stuff, you will pretty soon be alone on your page.

To maximise your returns on investment, have a Facebook strategy in place outlining what to post, how to engage your audience and when. The more interactive and engaging your Facebook page is the better, because every time somebody else interacts on your page all of their friends will see the interaction in their newsfeed. If ten people, with an average of 300 friends each, post something onto your wall, you could potentially have exposure to 3,000 people in the newsfeed. Of course, not everybody checks their newsfeed, but you get the picture.

Demand interaction by asking questions or encouraging people to share their comments and ideas. Make sure you reward them by thanking them for their thoughts and ideas. It should be a two-way street.

Another good Facebook strategy is to come up with certain topical days. Pick a day or two a week where you focus on one topic or area and, depending on your business, you post a relevant special tip or ask a question. Make it relevant to your business.

Here are some examples:

- **Inspirational Quote Monday**: Ask your fans to share their favourite quotes with you and your network.
- **Cleaning Tip Tuesday** (for a cleaning business): Post a cleaning tip and ask people to share their experiences.
- **Funny Friday**: Post a joke every Friday and get other people to share their jokes.

There are many more strategies to grow your fan base and leverage the power of Facebook for your business such as placing your Facebook URL in your marketing materials, email signature and putting a Facebook link on your website.

Add pictures of happy people using your product or services, maybe some team shots, a few product shots and some of you in action—anything that demonstrates that you are a fabulous business to work with.

There are a lot of great Facebook applications and one of them is the events feature. You can create an event on Facebook and then allow people to register online. If you are speaking at an event, exhibiting at an expo, running a workshop or organising an Open Day, create an event on Facebook and invite people online—it's very easy!

As with all of your marketing strategies, testing and measuring will help you to improve your Facebook strategies and work out what is best for your business. Facebook Analytics will help you do that by providing statistics on when people are active, how many have been interacting and what day of the week works best for your business. Very useful information.

It's your turn to take action

If you don't have a Facebook account yet, go to **www.facebook.com** and create your personal profile. You must own a personal profile to be able to create your business page, but you do not have to use your personal profile if you prefer not to.

Once you have created your account and you are logged in, you can create your business page. Just go to **www.facebook.com/pages/create.php**.

Your business page is 'owned' by your personal profile but is completely separate. So, don't fear. Your business fans do not have access to your personal profile and will not see those family photos or party pictures.

Make sure you swing by our page, 'Like' it and say hello. Just go to:

www.facebook.com/basicbananas

Twitter

Twitter is another free social networking and micro-blogging[29] service that allows you to interact with millions of people online. With the advancement of mobile  marketing, Twitter is great as people are tweeting from mobile devices from anywhere and everywhere. It is a fabulous instant communication tool to harness.

On Facebook you have 'fans' and on Twitter you have 'followers.' When finding people to follow, you

---

[29] Micro-blogging means that you can only share a short sentence as opposed to unlimited text. A tweet on Twitter can be up to 140 characters. A lot of 'tweeters' post personal stuff such as 'I just ate too much ice-cream,' 'I did a burp after drinking two beers,' 'I just washed all my undies.' Wow, isn't that interesting information (not!)?

can either find them by name or interests. This is quite powerful as you can follow people with similar interests, which is invaluable from a business perspective. For example, if you have a business selling golfing equipment, you can follow people who are interested in golf.

Twitter is another useful tool to do research with. You can find out what your target market talks about and what they want. You can also check out what your competitors are doing. Oh, and you can even stalk your favourite celebrities. Want to know what Lady Gaga, Oprah Winfrey or Justin Bieber is up to? Just follow them on Twitter (a sure way to waste a bit of time).

A lot of businesses use Twitter to interact with customers instantly and get instant feedback from them, providing fabulous customer service. For example, in 2011 when airports were closed due to volcanic ash, thousands of people were stranded and customer service phone lines could not handle all the enquiries. So, one airline jumped onto Twitter and provided excellent customer service, looking after their stranded passengers by keeping them updated immediately—and other airlines didn't. We will leave it up to you to guess which airline the passengers felt did a good job and which ones didn't.

> ### It's your turn to take action
>
> To get started on Twitter, go to **www.twitter.com** and follow the instructions to open your account. It will take around 5 minutes to have your account up and running. Post your first tweets and start following people by searching for their names.
>
> This is for the time-poor (Aren't we all?): If you'd like to automate Twitter and have your Facebook posts go directly onto your Twitter as well, you can connect those two. So, when you write something onto Facebook, it will automatically also be a tweet on Twitter. To do that, log in to both Twitter and Facebook and go to www.facebook.com/twitter, and you are a few clicks away from automating your Twitter.

Twitter also makes it possible for your clients to post about their experiences with your business straight away and let all of their followers know how good you are. And let's face it, we all love talking about the latest great gadget or service we bought that has helped us. In this way, Twitter can give you access to a whole new demographic market and drive more traffic to your website.

Twitter also has some great functions to test and measure. For example, as mentioned, you can see when somebody has 'tweeted' about your business and what they are saying about you. It's not just for twits.

You Tube

Video marketing is a sure way to get results fast. Online video will help you create awareness, build trust with your prospects and drive traffic to your website where you can capture their details and build relationships, as discussed earlier.

Many of our business enquiries, and that of our clients, come through YouTube. The prospects have come across our videos and checked a few out, which helped build familiarity and trust that in turn led the prospect to our website. The videos did the job for us. Don't you just love good marketing systems?

Although getting more and more crowded, it is still relatively easy to get your videos ranked high in search engines by using the right **keywords**. A higher ranking means better visibility in a search engine, more viewers and ultimately more traffic to your website.

Google actually owns YouTube and places videos from YouTube in its search results. So, if somebody is searching for a plumber in Oceanville, by 'googling' 'Oceanville plumber,' Google will search for anything online named 'Oceanville plumber.' If a plumber created a video called 'Oceanville plumber,' his video would then show up in the Google search results for the person to view if there is not a lot of competition for those keywords. This is basically free advertising!

Sounds easy? Well, it is pretty easy. Why do so many people shy away from creating videos then? Probably because they do not like being in front of a camera, think it's too hard to create their own short clips or imagine creating a video will break the bank. The reality is you do not have to spend thousands of dollars on professionally filmed and edited videos and hope to win a prize at the Cannes Film Festival. Filming your short video clips on a handy cam is totally fine, or you can even use your iPhone. Then all you need is a computer to download the videos and put them onto the internet.

Regarding your fear of being in front of the camera, no worries; you can also film your screen by using a screen capturing software. No excuses!

What sort of content do you put into the videos? Well, you can be as creative as you want, but to help you get started, what about sharing some valuable insider tips? You could also show people around your business, explaining certain parts of the production of your products or how your services work. You can also get your customers to talk about you, how they have used your products and services, and how they absolutely loved them. Not all of your clients will want to talk in front of your handy cam, but you'll see that some do love it and can't wait to get in front of the camera. So, instead of a written testimonial, you can get a videoed one.

Once you have got your video all ready to go, you need to publish it on YouTube.

Google relies on what you have named your video and your description to know when to make it appear for a viewer. For example, if someone searches 'How to save money on your electricity bill' and you have a video with the same name, bingo, you just got a free advertisement. And it will be shown to someone who is actually interested in what you have to say.

'How to' videos are very popular, so create your own such as 'How to get a six pack,' 'How to make a carrot cake,' 'How to get rid of a headache' or 'How to remove a wine stain from your carpet.'

It's your turn to take action

1. Set up your own YouTube channel by going to **www.youtube.com**.
2. Then film five or so short videos (3 – 5 minutes in length is perfect), and give them different names to test and measure which keywords work best in your industry.

3. Upload your videos onto your YouTube channel. In your description of the video make sure you add a Call to Action to send viewers to your website (for example 'For more free tips on xxxx go to http://www.mywebsite.com'). A little tip here: Placing http://www before your URL will create a live, clickable link to your website.

Et voila, you are officially an online video marketer. Now you just need to test and measure your results by checking which videos are getting the most views and make adjustments to your titles and descriptions as you go.

LinkedIn

LinkedIn is a professional networking tool that works particularly (but not exclusively) well for business-to-business (B2B)[30]. relationships. It is like a directory of valuable business contacts and, just as with 'offline' networking, you get to choose who to connect with. LinkedIn allows you to find people

---

[30] B2B or business-to-business refers to transactions between businesses rather than from a business to consumers. So, if your business is providing products or services to other businesses, you are in a B2B relationship.

based on their profession, keywords, companies, education and so on, which makes it an extremely effective tool.

LinkedIn has great Search Engine Optimisation and ranks very high on Google. So, when you search for a name on Google or any other search engine, you will usually come across that person's LinkedIn profile (if they have one). LinkedIn is great to show off your many talents (Come on, don't be humble now!).

Just as with most other social media tools, LinkedIn is all about give and take. It does take a bit of work (10 minutes a day) to get best results. It is not enough to just have your LinkedIn profile up and wait for something to happen. You need to engage in it actively to get results by participating in groups, sharing your knowledge and connecting with people.

An extremely powerful LinkedIn feature is that your clients can **leave recommendations** on your profile, which provides instant social proof and makes you more appealing to prospects when they look at your profile and work history. Imagine if you are looking for an accountant on LinkedIn and you find two in your local area, but one of them has a lot of recommendations and the other doesn't. Which one would you choose to contact?

To get recommendations, remember to also recommend businesses you have liked working with instead of just hoping to be endorsed. It's all about give and take.

LinkedIn's potential is huge. People can find you based on the **keywords** that you use, and likewise you can search for potential strategic alliance partners, find people with similar interests and email people directly without having to go through numerous channels.

Our clients also love using it to do research about people when preparing for meetings. For example, if you are about to meet the CEO of Goldmine, you can look him up on LinkedIn and find out more about him before your meeting. A lot of recruitment companies are using LinkedIn to find suitable candidates.

Another underestimated feature of LinkedIn is its **groups**. There are thousands of groups on LinkedIn where people discuss different topics. A great strategy is to join and participate in group discussions that your target market is part of. Demonstrate your expertise and position yourself as the expert in your niche. You will certainly build trust and attract more business. Or you could even create your own LinkedIn group and invite people to join it.

It's your turn to take action

Create your LinkedIn profile by going to **www.linkedin.com**.

Make sure your profile is complete. Add a photo (preferably not one of you dressed up as a clown, unless that's your profession), fill in your work experiences, skills, specialties, etc. Make sure you use relevant keywords so you can be found easily. Join a few groups and start participating in the discussions.

10

More online marketing strategies

Cyber love

"Give a person a fish and you feed them for a day; teach that person to use the Internet and they won't bother you for weeks."

~ UNKNOWN

AFTER FABIO MENTIONED THAT GIRLS LIKE MEN WITH pupppy dogs, Matt went to his local animal shelter and adopted two little puppies. This will surely turn heads, he thought. Plus, he figured he was making a difference in the life of two dogs that did not have a home.

It didn't take Matt long to fall in love with his two

puppies, which he named Mickey and Minnie. They were a great distraction from Anna and girls in general. He didn't know a thing about dogs, so he started searching for information about puppy training and other dog-related topics online. He came across an online dog training course. He even found a podcast for dog owners, a forum and an iPhone app explaining what the different dog sounds mean. There was so much information that Matt felt a bit overwhelmed.

Meanwhile, Mickey and Minnie were chewing Matt's converse shoes.

There is no doubt that the online world is growing fast—very fast—even more so with **mobile marketing**, which means people are accessing the internet from their mobile devices such as the iPhone and the iPad. You can try to put your head in the sand like an ostrich waiting for it to pass—but the problem is it won't! The younger generations especially are doing almost everything online: chatting to friends, shopping, meeting their future wife or husband, learning to do something or just killing time[31] at work.

Considering that these young people will most likely be your future customers, you must hang out where they are—online. You can either hate it or see it as a great opportunity for your small business to

---

[31] 'Killing time' is nothing criminal; it means to waste time

gain exposure to a much broader audience without having to have a million dollar budget. The second option will be more profitable for your business.

Small businesses usually do not have a $500k budget for national TV ads, but they now can go online and gain exposure to an international market. With the net, the world is your oyster. The World Wide Web offers you access to the whole world, so the possibilities are unlimited.

The biggest advantage with an online business, as opposed to offline, is that you can fail very cheaply. What we mean is you can test and measure without blowing your life savings. If something does not work, get a mentor, ask for advice, make some changes and just try again. In this case, it really is *'What have you got to lose?'* You can create an online business for a few hundred dollars, or even less, depending on how you set it up. The point is you can test things without it costing you the world.

So jump on the bandwagon and don't just enjoy the ride; harness the power of the internet to your ultimate advantage. If you are feeling a little disoriented or have some 'performance anxiety,' don't worry. Ask somebody to walk you through the maze of online marketing strategies out there.

We have already taken you through some social media sites (Facebook, Twitter, LinkedIn and YouTube). But there are so many other online marketing strategies you can adopt as a small business, it's worthy of a whole book. In this chapter we will look at a few of them.

Remember, though, not all work for every business. It's best to **test, measure and implement** the ones that give you the best return on investment.

A quick word of warning here; there are a lot of shonky [32] online marketers out there that might promise you that you can sit in your undies and make millions without lifting a finger. The truth is that you will still need to lift a finger or two to set it all up and make it work. Sorry to crush your dream but there is definitely no Get Rich Quick schemes that work. If someone is promising you millions within two days, you better grab your wallet and run as fast as you can.

Now, let's look at some cracker online marketing strategies.

Pay per click advertising

Google Adwords used to be, and still is, a very popular and easy way to drive traffic to your website or landing page. A few years ago, it was relatively cheap to use Google Adwords to send millions of people to your website or product pages.

You can see Google Ads when you search for something on **www.google.com** and, depending on your search terms, there will be sponsored ads at the

---

[32] 'Shonky' means dodgy or poor quality

very top and bottom of your page. These are ads you pay for every time someone clicks on them. So, if you want to appear at the top without Search Engine Optimisation (SEO), you can set up some Google Adwords for your relevant keywords. (SEO is discussed further down in this chapter).

Because of its popularity and success, Google Adwords has become more and more competitive and therefore more and more expensive for small businesses to use. It is still an effective tool, but you must make sure you study how to use it effectively, test and measure your results and/or get an expert to help you out. Otherwise, you could end up spending a lot of money.

The advantages of Google Ads are you only pay when people click on your ad and you can start small with a prepaid balance while you test and measure your results.

Jess, one of our clients, is using Google Adwords very effectively. She runs sales skills trainings and workshops and mainly fills her workshops using Google Adwords. She simply turns her campaigns on when she needs participants and makes sure her expenses are lower than her sales.

To find out more about how to use Google Adwords, head over to **www.adwords.google.com**.

Facebook Ads are another pay per click method. Similar to Google Adwords, you pay when somebody clicks on your ad, or you can pay per view. You can find Facebook ads on the right side of your Facebook page and in the newsfeed. Again, they can be quite targeted as you can choose what type of profile you want them to appear on, according to demographics and interests. If you sold baby food, for example, you could target mums specifically. Or if you sold yoga DVDs, you could make your ads show up on people's profiles that have yoga under interests.

Search engine optimisation (SEO) for organic ranking

Wow, that's a mouthful of 'techy' words! Let us explain. When you search for something online using a search engine like Google, the search engine will do its best to show you the most relevant information on the web in regards to what you are searching for with your keywords.

The process to optimise your website so that it appears higher in the rankings for certain words or phrases is what is called **Search Engine Optimisation** (SEO).

Let's say you run a hotel in Port Stephens called Salt and Sun Hotel. When people search for accommodation in Port Stephens, what would they search for? If they didn't know the name of Salt and Sun Hotel they wouldn't search for it and would search using a phrase like 'accommodation in Port Stephens.' If your website isn't optimised to appear for a search term like this, then potential clients will never find you.

We do not want to get too techy here, but think of the words your potential clients are using to search online for a product like yours and put them on your website—in the titles and main content. This will be a good start to give your website a little boost up the rankings.

There is a very useful tool called the *Google Keyword Planner* that will help you find out how many people are searching for certain words or phrases and if there is a lot of competition, and it will give you other alternative suggestions. To find the Google Keyword Planner just go to www.google.com and search for that term and it will come up.

You can do some basic SEO tasks yourself by using the right keywords, but it is probably best to outsource it to someone who knows what they are doing, so you can focus on what you are good at. There is a range of providers out there charging anything from a couple of hundred dollars to thousands of dollars per month. If they have achieved great results for their clients, they should know what they say they know.

Online directories

There are literally hundreds of online directories for your business to be listed on for free or some are paid. Again, besides having more online exposure, it will also help your search engine ranking.

When search engines like Google see that there are lots of links to your website from other websites, it thinks you must be very popular (which of course you are) and improves your ranking. It's like in high school when you hang out with the cool kids; you are suddenly perceived as a cool kid.

It is pretty easy to list your business online. Just go to a search engine such as Google and search for 'free online business directory,' and you will find a lot of options. A good place to start is Google Places and True Local.

Blogging

If you like writing (even if you don't), start your own blog or add one to your website. Why? Because it shows that you are an expert in your industry and the search engines love new content on a website.

There are a few things you need to think about:

- You can either have your blog on a separate website or as part of your normal site. We prefer having them as part of your website as the search

engines will reward you for having new content on your site.
- Using relevant keywords in your blog posts helps your site rank higher.
- Your posts can be as short or as long as you deem appropriate. Even a few lines are better than nothing.
- Allow your readers to engage with you and leave comments. It not only builds a community, Google rewards interaction on a site.
- Think about guest blogging for other blogs and adding links back to your website to bring you more traffic. All you have to do is approach relevant blogs and ask the owner if they would like to publish your articles for free.

Article distribution

We love leveraging our work, so let's take those blog posts (or articles) and distribute them online. Posting them online is an awesome way to get yourself out there and attract a heap of links back to your website, which also helps your organic ranking.

There are many article distribution channels that will do the job for you. Just 'google' search 'article distribution' and you will find a lot of options.

iPhone and iPad applications (apps)

In the first quarter of 2011, Apple Mac sold over 16 million iPhones and over 7 million iPads. The iPad was the fastest selling consumer electronics item in history! With this amazing technological evolution came applications (apps). Each month hundreds of thousands of apps are sold, and some people are making serious money by creating their own applications. An app or application is a software program you can download onto your mobile device like any other program on your computer.

Why not develop your own application and gain access to a huge database through iTunes where they are being sold?

How do you make money with apps? Buyers can either purchase your app, so you make some extra cash, or they can download it for free. Free apps are very popular, and you could develop an upsell of a more advanced version that is available for a small cost.

ITunes looks after the whole sales process and takes a commission. The good news is that you can send customers a direct message to promote other products or upsell to a better version of what they have already got. Besides the money aspect, an app provides you with great exposure and access to a whole different market, which can be even more important than making money with it.

Think about whether an app would be beneficial for your business. The possibilities are endless. There are apps that check the weather, teach you guitar lessons, do special calculations for builders and give you a surf report... The sky is the limit!

Podcasting

Podcasting [33] —online audio or video shows—is another great way to educate your market and be perceived as the expert in your niche. A podcast is basically your own online radio show that people can subscribe to and listen to in their own time.

Setting up your own podcast is pretty simple; you just need to figure out what your strategy is and what you want to talk about on your show. Great content is a must for your podcast to be successful. You could share valuable tips, tricks, interviews and information—business related or not. It helps when your target market is interested. Like any radio or TV show, make it fun and entertaining for the listener. Remember how we spoke about the character of you and your brand earlier? Well, this is

---

[33] The word 'podcast' is derived from 'broadcast' and 'pod,' as in iPod, because podcasts are often listened to on portable devices such as the iPod or the iPhone

where you can bring it out, whether it is serious, cheeky, funny, quirky or weird.

Podcasting is a great tool to attract your prospects, create trust and turn them into raving fans. It's a great word-of-mouth tool as your listeners will spread the word for you if your podcast is worth listening to.

For our popular podcast we conduct twenty to thirty minute interviews with inspirational business owners where they share their secrets to their success with our listeners. If you go to iTunes and search for 'Basic Bananas,' you will find our podcast. Subscribe to it so you keep up to date with the most recent interviews, and please leave a comment if you like what you listen to.

Email marketing

We have already touched on email marketing in *Chapter 6 Building Relationships*. Once you have a database full of prospects who have chosen to opt in to what you have to offer, you can think about doing the occasional product or service launch via your emails. Just make sure not to do them too frequently or you will annoy your contacts. One of our clients, who sells yoga courses, has turned her business around by doing email campaigns. We created a series of emails launching a new course that came with a special for her database for a limited time only. This is highly effective if you have a good database and an excellent product or service to launch.

Webinars

Running webinars (online live classes) is great to leverage your time and get yourself in front of many people all at once (the power of speaking to many people instead of one by one). You don't even have to get out of your pyjamas to run a webinar.

Webinars are also fabulous to add value to your clients. You can do them for free as a bonus, make them part of your packages or sell them as an additional product.

The process of running your own webinars is pretty simple and goes like this: Pick a topic and title for your class, choose a date and time, then set up the webinar using a program such as www.gotowebinar.com. There are a few different providers but this is the one we are using. Then email people the invitation with a link to register for the class. At a set time, they will click the link to join you. Once viewers join, they can see your screen, hear your voice and post questions. You can even unmute listeners if you want to talk to them directly. It is just like being in a classroom, but people can be anywhere in the world as long as they have a computer and internet. Some distance learning courses are using webinars now too.

We run webinars for our clients from all over the world, and there's no difference whether we are in the same suburb or on the other side of the globe. The only difference is the 'time difference,' and we have had to run classes in the middle of the night because we were in a different time zone. In terms of locations, we have run them from the weirdest places while travelling overseas. Some of them included a busy bar in Indonesia, in the back of a campervan in Spain and on top of a mountain in Switzerland. As long as there is a good internet connection you can be anywhere!

Besides teaching something valuable, online classes are a fantastic way to build relationships and move prospects to the next step with you. Instead of giving them a huge sales pitch, you provide value, answer questions and let them become familiar with you and your products and services. You can even make a special offer at the end of a class to reward your listeners and get them to take action.

For your webinar to be successful you have to invite people to attend, otherwise it might become quite a lonely affair. If you have a database (list of clients, potential clients, past clients), invite them all to your webinar to re-connect or upsell. You can also invite people via your social media networks by posting the invite link for people to register. Do not worry if your first class only has two people in it (even if they are your mother and brother). Persist and your numbers will increase.

Ask other business owners if they would be happy to invite their database contacts to a webinar you are running. Depending on your arrangement with other business owners, you can offer a kickback for the other business for any sales made. Let's say another business invites their database to your webinar and ten people become clients of yours; you could offer the referring business a commission.

Many of our clients are experiencing massive business growth because they have such a wide reach with the use of webinars. Tania, one of our clients who runs Quantum Reading courses, offers her courses via webinars to people in Australia, the US and the Caribbean!

It's your turn to take action

Go through each of the strategies listed in this chapter and implement one per month (or per week if you are on the fast track!). Think about which methods will be most effective and beneficial for your target market. You do not have to do them all; just start off with one. Do it well. Systemise and automate it, and then go to the next one.

Lumpy mail

Love letters with a little something extra!

*"What a lot we lost when we stopped writing letters.
You can't re-read a phone call."*

~ Liz Carpenter

MATT GOT MORE AND MORE DESPERATE TO SEE Anna again and decided to do something about it, rather than just wait and hope to hear from her. One morning on his way to work, he stopped at the news agency and asked the lady at the counter if she had any cute cards for a girl he liked.

"Hmmm, let me think. What's the purpose of the card? Is it to fix something or to impress?" The lady had a slight French accent, and she didn't seem to really care that there were about seven people waiting to be served. She had all the time in the world and certainly loved her job. She was focusing on one customer at a time, just like a French lady in the village bakery, explaining all the different treats to her customers... while ten people are waiting to be served.

"Impressing someone would be the right expression I guess." For some reason Matt felt like telling the lady about Anna. "I met this girl," Matt said, lowering his voice, "and I like her and would love to see her again."

"I've got an idea for you then! This is what a French gentleman would do to impress. You know our French men are very romantic!" The lady gave Matt a proud smile. "We've got some cute invitations for a romantic dinner. Why don't you cook a delicious dinner for the girl? Make an effort and spend a day or so in the kitchen to impress! C'est magnifique! Maybe some horse fillet with a special French sauce. I can copy a recipe if you'd like. I've got the most amazing recipe book."

"Thank you, but I might pass on that one. We don't really eat horse here in Australia," said Matt, laughing. "I'll buy the card though; great idea. Maybe I can make a Shepherd's Pie[34] instead!" Matt got his wallet out and paid. Meanwhile, the line behind him had grown to about twelve customers.

In his lunch break Matt wrote the card for Anna, inviting her over for dinner. He was a bit nervous about her possible reaction but thought it was worth a try. So he popped it in the post.

---

[34] A Shepherd's Pie is a pie with minced beef and potato on top.

Two weeks later, Matt still hadn't heard from Anna. Was it too much too fast? Wondering what he did wrong, he went over to Fabio's office to ask for help.

Fabio was in a meeting with one of his creative teams but waved Matt in and told him to wait for five minutes until he was done. "What's up, mate?" Fabio leaned back in his chair and crossed his legs, looking as neat as always.

"Nothing much to be honest. Just been working and trying to impress Anna. Not much happening on that front though. I sent her a card to invite her for dinner but haven't heard back yet."

"Well done for taking action! That sounds like a great idea to me. If she doesn't want to come, I'll come over. What's on the menu?" Matt wondered how Fabio could always be so cheerful, sometimes annoyingly cheerful.

"Jokes aside, did you have a Call to Action or RSVP on your card, asking her to give you a call or text to confirm a day?" Fabio asked.

"Hmmm not really, I think I just said that I wanted to invite her over. I didn't really ask her to call me. Maybe I should call her..."

"Well, maybe you should, but let's get a few things right first," Fabio suggested as he got up and started walking up and down his office. He looked like a university professor searching for the right words.

"You work in advertising and the marketing principles you use for your clients here also apply to this. Firstly, you must have a Call to Action to get any response at all! Secondly, you know from your direct mail campaigns that a mail-out with something in the envelope (or what we call 'lumpy mail') is much more effective than a card in a flat envelope—the reason being that 'normal' envelopes look like bills and advertising. Most people open their mail over the recycle bin, so you need to send something that stands out a bit to avoid it being dumped."

Fabio opened his drawer and took out a padded envelope with a mouse matt in it. "Isn't it cooler to receive something like this in the mail rather than just a card? This campaign was for one of our hotel chains. On the mouse pad it says 'You are only one click away from having an amazing holiday!' Do you remember this campaign? It was really successful. Every time someone at work (who'd received the mail-out) was bored, they'd see this little ad and start looking at holiday destinations. Clever, huh?"

"Yeah, I remember." Matt's mind was going at 200 miles an hour, thinking about how he could apply this to his campaign to win over Anna without looking like a dipstick (A 'dipstick' is Aussie slang for an idiot or loser).

"I got it!" he said, a notch too loud. "I'm going to send her a spoon and a fork and tell her to bring them to dinner and that I'll provide the rest!"

Fabio was laughing out loud. "That is actually quite a bloody awesome idea. It's quirky and funny. Pretty risky business, but I like your style. Either way, at least it will have an impact. Make sure you include a Call to Action this time!" Fabio's cell phone started ringing.

"What about something like, 'I am free on Friday or Saturday. Just send me a text message to confirm the day and I'll be ready with dinner. PS: Don't forget to bring the cutlery.'" Matt said.

"Yep, sounds good!" Fabio picked up his cell phone and gave Matt a thumbs-up. Matt was excited and a little nervous at the same time. Something had to happen!

Targeted 'lumpy mail' (an envelope with an object in it which makes it 'lumpy') is a highly effective strategy to generate qualified leads for a small business. Its success really depends on the right approach, the right market and the right message. Just like Matt, you have to be creative and 'stand-outish' so that your campaign has a positive impact, gets people to take action and makes them remember you. Something quirky, cheeky or funny, yet professional, usually works well.

As Fabio discussed above, lumpy mail is much more effective than just a flat letter because it will stand out from all the other mail your prospect is receiving every day and doesn't look like a bill. The good thing about a direct mail campaign is that while our email inboxes get more and more crowded by the day, our letterboxes don't. It used to be so exciting to go to the letterbox and find some cards or letters in the mail. How good is it when you get a little present in the mail? Nowadays there is usually not much more in there than a few flyers and bills.

Find a gift that links in with your message or the reason for your letter rather than just sending random gifts without tying it in with your marketing approach.

Here's a tip: To find inspiration, go down to the dollar shop and see what gadgets are available and how they could work with your campaign.

Who do you send lumpy mail to? A good place to start is to get a list of people in the industry or demographic category you want to target. You can either buy a list from a list broker (just be sure it is a high quality list), get your assistant or VA (virtual assistant) to compile a list of people you would like to approach or send it to your existing database of prospects.

Send the campaign only to a segment of your database, and then test and measure your results. Then adjust it if necessary to maximise your efforts.

The most important thing to make or break this strategy is that you must give them a **follow-up call**. This can increase your conversion rate massively. Unfortunately, a lot of businesses send out great lumpy mail but never follow up because they are either lazy, scared or don't know what to say. The good thing about sending your prospects a gift in your lumpy mail is that you do have something to talk about! Just ask them whether they have received it and enjoyed it.

A lot of recipients will open your envelope, enjoy your letter and think it's a great idea, but will put it into their 'to-do' piles where it gets buried under other important things, never to be done. By you being proactive and giving them a call, they will be grateful because it gives them the opportunity to ask any questions they might have about your products or services without their having to call you or send you an email. This is called 'warm calling' rather than 'cold calling,' and is much more fun and effective.

Let's look at a few examples of successful lumpy mail campaigns some of our clients have run on a small budget. This strategy doesn't have to cost thousands of dollars. It can be very low cost and high return for you.

Example 1: The quirky gift

With Petra, a marketing manager of a plant rental business, we decided to get involved with events managers to help them decorate their events with beautiful plants. The lumpy mail consisted of a letter and a beautiful bamboo stick that could be put into a cup of water and placed onto an otherwise boring desk in an office environment—a nice little gift.

A few days after sending out the campaign, Petra called the recipients and said something like "I just wanted to make sure the bamboo stick arrived all healthy and happy." Her humour was a great icebreaker and a completely different approach to that of a lot of cold-callers. Everyone who received a phone call to check how the bamboo was going absolutely loved the present and said the bamboo was going okay. The funny thing is that some of the sticks arrived a bit sad as it was a hot summer's day. (Note: Make sure you do not send chocolates in the middle of summer. Unless your clients like licking chocolate off an envelope, it might not be the best idea; although it would give them something to talk about!) The bamboo stick campaign was very successful and Petra picked up some big clients.

Example 2: The gift with a special message

Rita, a gorgeous client who owns a children's play centre, sent a stress ball to children's vacation care centres, inviting them to drop the children at her play centre for a day to de-stress and relax over a cup of coffee. Another clever and successful campaign.

Example 3: The ol' $1 bill trick

A method that has had great success in the USA is sending a one dollar note (shame there are no $1 Aussie bills) attached to letters, explaining *'This won't be the first time you will receive money if you decide to work with me*' or '*I've attached this dollar bill for two reasons; one is to get your attention and the second is because I will show you ways to uncover plenty more of these within your business.*' This campaign works particularly well for accountants, business coaches and financial planners. One of our clients, Todd, a business coach, has sent out a fake million dollar bill to his target market using the above strategy and picked up some new clients.

Exactly three days after sending out his lumpy mail to Anna, Matt got a text from her saying, 'Next Saturday, 7pm your place. I'll bring the spoon and fork and you organise the rest!' Matt was so excited he dropped his iPhone. He quickly picked it up, gave it a clean with his fancy new shirt and read the message over and over again. His lumpy mail had worked! Anna was coming over for dinner. He was so happy he literally could not wipe the smile off his face, like a very proud French baker who had just created the perfect baguette.

It's your turn to take action

1. Think about who you want to target with your lumpy mail campaign. What are your objectives?
2. Find the lump—something you can send out with your mail and ties in with your message.
3. Write the letter or card that goes with your lump. Personalise it by using the recipient's first name.
4. Choose a segment of your target base to trial the lumpy mail with.
5. Follow up with a phone call.
6. Test and measure your results, adjust the campaign and send it to the next segment.

12

The power of events and seminars

It's party time!

"After all, what is your host's purpose in having a party? Surely not for you to enjoy yourself; if that were their sole purpose, they'd have simply sent champagne and women over to your place by taxi."

~ P.J. O'ROURKE

MATT HAD A REALLY NICE DINNER WITH ANNA THAT Saturday night. He was more nervous than when he had sat his final exams at university ten years before. Everything went pretty smooth except for dropping some red wine on the fancy rug he bought in Bali the year before. Normally, he would have freaked out, but on this occasion he couldn't have cared less.

Afterwards, Anna suggested they have a night out with their mutual friends. Matt offered to organise a party at his place, even though he normally didn't like to have too many people over at his new apartment. But he would do anything to impress her.

Matt couldn't wait until Monday to tell Fabio all about his romantic first date with Anna. So, he called him on Sunday. Fabio sounded sleepy and crusty.

"My wife and kids are visiting my in-laws for the weekend, so I went out with a few mates and didn't get home until a sparrow's fart[35]. What's up anyway? Why are you calling so early and on a Sunday?"

Matt looked at the big clock in the kitchen. It was nearly midday, not so early!

"I had dinner with Anna last night and it went really well! She didn't stay over, but I think that's okay—you told me not to rush things! Anyway, she suggested we have a night out with friends, and I promised to organise a party at my place next weekend. Are you in? I need some male support!"

"I'm not partying or drinking anymore after last night, but if you promise to have heaps of cordial, I'll be there! By the way, I forgot to let you know about this other strategy, but it looks like you got onto it by yourself anyway."

"What are you talking about?" Matt was intrigued.

"Well, we call this technique 'one to many' or 'the power of many.'"

---

[35] Have you ever heard a bird fart? We haven't. But 'sparrow's fart' is a saying meaning very early in the morning at daybreak. Apparently birds fart when they first wake up... hmmm.

"Which technique? Am I using a technique?" Matt chuckled.

"Yes, you are, Matt. And it's one of my favourite ones too! Instead of having meetings with thirty people to find out whether they want what you've got, businesses run seminars or talks where they invite prospects to come along to find out more about the product or service and its benefits. It works really well for a lot of businesses as long as the event is fun and there are many benefits for attending. It can't be just a big sales pitch or people won't come," explained Fabio.

"Hmmm, sounds interesting, and I can see how it could work well to find girls. All I would do is throw a fun party and get all of my friends to bring lots of girls. But now that I've already selected my 'client,' it's a bit too late. I think this would have worked really well when I was looking for someone. Although you never know, suddenly one of her friends could be even more interesting."

Fabio groaned. "Oh, man. What happened to the lovely Matt I met a few months ago?"

"Just kidding," Matt replied quickly.

"So when is that dinner party of yours?" asked a tired sounding Fabio. "This Friday!" responded Matt, faster than a rat up a drain pipe. "I'll reserve a seat for you Fabio."

This strategy of 'one to many' works really well for most small businesses. As Fabio mentioned, the main benefit is being able to speak to a group of people at once rather than spending your time meeting thirty people individually. (Yes, there still is value in meeting people individually, but your time is limited and this strategy is business meetings on steroids). Running events will also help you filter out people that would not have been a good match for your business anyway. Many of our clients use this process to weed out any time-wasters[36]. So, instead of spending a lot of time with people that will never spend a cent with you, they can come to your seminars if they are interested. And if they like your stuff, they can purchase. If not, that's okay too.

Running events will also help you gain access to an audience you might otherwise not have had access to because your prospects will most likely bring along friends and colleagues if you ask them to, given that you offer lots of value. This again will help you grow your database. Just make sure you **grab everyone's details** at the event and ask for permission to send them your emails.

Leverage your efforts and make your event a recurring one so that your past attendees can refer others to join you at the next one. It is like a

---

[36] A time waster is someone who takes your time away from focusing on achieving your vision and mission. There are always those who take a lot of your time with only little or no return. You need to save your energy for the good prospects and clients so you can provide them with the best possible service.

snowball effect; once you have got about sixty or so past attendees, it will become easier and easier to book out your next event as people will refer others if they find that you are providing lots of value. All you will need to do is send out the occasional email announcing your next event and ask them to pass on the invitation to their friends, family and colleagues.

Make sure you look after your attendees, providing water, coffee and tea, and maybe some snacks. Apparently love goes through the stomach.

Now let's look at the **different types of events** you could hold for your business, depending on your product or service, target market and your objectives.

TYPES OF EVENTS

Talks

This one is very popular for businesses that can talk about a topic that their prospects would find interesting and useful. The purpose of these talks is not to just sell something, but to educate and get attendees to walk out with new ideas and solutions to a problem. It is important to honour people's time.

Obviously, you will make them an offer to buy something at the end; it would be rude not to. But do not only make it about the sale or people will not come back. A talk is really **about providing value,**

educating people about a certain topic and **giving them some cool 'tools'** to walk away with. This strategy works especially well for natural health practitioners, doctors, optometrists, financial advisors, mortgage brokers, accountants, consultants and other service providers.

Karla, a life coach, barely made any money when she first joined our programs. One of the strategies we helped her implement was to regularly run talks as she had a huge knowledge about the human mind and what makes people tick. At her first event she only had a handful of participants. But as she was purely focusing on providing a lot of amazing information and how-to's, past participants started recommending her. And now her monthly talks are booked out every time. This one strategy has helped her turn around her business within a couple of months.

If you are scared of talking or do not like to talk in front of a group of people, you can also get a guest speaker—a well-known one in the industry would be a double bonus. Or attend a public speaking course.

Let's look at some topic ideas to get you started:

- Stylist: *How to look and feel a million dollars with your current wardrobe.*
- Landscaper: *How to make your neighbours envy your garden.*
- Carpenter: *How to make your floors last forever.*
- Accountant: *How to save thousands of dollars on your tax bill.*
- Web designer: *How to make your website work for you 24/7.*
- Business coach: *How to double your business in less than 12 months.*
- Hairdresser: *10 styling tips to look like a celebrity in less than 10 minutes.*

Workshops

Another similar event type is a workshop. The only difference is the event is usually a bit longer than a talk; 2-3 hours is perfect (whereas a talk might only go for one hour). You can set it up as a workshop where your participants take a pen and paper and work on certain things. Depending on your target market, you either hold the workshops early in the morning, during the day or in the evening. Generally, early mornings and evenings work well for a lot of our clients.

Family event

This one works really well if your target markets are families, parents or children. You could organise different activities for families to attend, which will give your business exposure and get new people through the door. For example, if you own a child care centre, you could organise a family afternoon with lots of fun kids' activities. Or if you own a family practice, you could invite families over to learn about the body and healthy habits by playing games and involving the kids. On another note, if your target market is families, a smart thing to do is to make your business very kids-friendly and maybe have a play corner with toys, games and books for the children. If you look after the children, they will be the ones wanting to come back. Do not underestimate the power of persuasion of a child!

Business event

Again, this one works well if you work in a B2B environment. You could organise a business networking and information night where you invite other businesses to come along to network and to also learn something new from a special guest speaker. Businesses love every opportunity to network, and if you present, you will be seen as the expert and the go-to guy on your subject.

Multi speaker event

This is another great strategy to gain access to a much wider audience. Form a strategic alliance with other businesses that have the same target market but sell a different product or service and have something interesting to say. Then you all invite your contacts to a fabulous night of educational content and great networking opportunities. For example, if you are a personal trainer, you could ask your local chiropractor and life coach whether they would like to run an event with you, with each of you inviting your clients and prospects. You each then get to share some great content for about twenty minutes, and at the end of your spiel you make a special offer. The beauty about this event is that you all get exposure to people you otherwise would not have.

Fundraising

What about using this occasion to make a difference and support a good cause? Or you could organise a special fundraising event and invite your clients and prospects for a delicious dinner with all funds going to a project you want to support.

This is not only a feel-good exercise; you will also be perceived as the guy/girl who makes a difference in the community. Your business might become the preferred choice for your prospects as it is more appealing to support someone who is contributing to society. Let's think about it for a moment. When you go to the supermarket to buy a bottle of water and you see two similar bottles at the same price, but one bottle supports a charity and one doesn't, which one will you most likely choose? The one that is supporting a good cause, of course.

Open fun day

Open days used to be more common in the good ol' days, but it is still a very effective strategy if you make your day fun and worthwhile. You can combine any of the above suggestions to make your open day a success. Make sure your open day is not just a big advertising exercise. Make it interactive, engaging and fun, and most importantly make sure you collect people's details for your database. You could run a competition and collect details this way.

You can also allow your visitors to trial your services or products. Trialing or sampling is a very effective, low-cost way for your prospects to fall in love with your stuff.

So depending on your objectives, your target market's needs, and your products or services, you can choose any of the above event types or even a combination of a few. The best way to find out what works for your business is to give something a go.

The following Friday, Matt threw his dinner party. Well, it wasn't much of a party really. Matt was glad Fabio joined him as he struggled to find suitable friends to come. So he settled with Fabio only and Anna brought two girlfriends. Matt cooked some bangers[37] on the Barbie[38] and prepared some exotic salads, thinking it would make him look like husband material. The night was pretty uneventful, but they all had a good time and the girls did admire Matt's culinary skills. It was worth the effort!

It's your turn to take action

1. Think about the purpose for your event.
2. Pick one type of event, keeping in mind your target market and what they like.
3. Organise it and invite your prospects to join you. Please do not expect thousands of people to join you at the first one (unless you are some sort of celebrity or have a huge database of prospects). If you do a fantastic job, your participants will spread the word for you and things will snowball.

---

[37] 'Bangers' is an Aussie word for sausages.
[38] 'Barbie' is not to be confused with the Barbie doll. 'Barbie' is short for barbecue in Australia.

4. Test and measure by asking your participants for feedback.
5. Do it all over again!

13

Teaming up

You are not alone!

"Coming together is a beginning, staying together is progress and working together is success."

~ Henry Ford

TWO WEEKS PASSED AND MATT AND FABIO HAD lunch at a small Spanish tapas bar in town. Different fresh and not-so-fresh tapas were displayed behind a glass counter.

"Not much has happened yet with Anna," Matt started. "I haven't had the courage to ask her out since the BBQ, but we have been sending each other text messages. What should I do next?" He looked at Fabio, hoping for some advice.

Fabio threw a small piece of bread with something that looked like fish into his mouth, only to spit it out straight away. "That's disgusting. I better get a cup of vino to wash this thing down." Matt grinned.

"This Anna-thing has been going on forever, Matt. Are you sure Anna's 'the one?' The waters are looking a little murky. Are you ready to try something else to get things a bit clearer?"

"Sure. Ready spaghetti," Matt said, only realising how stupid he sounded after saying it.

"Maybe you need to play a little more, just to see whether Anna is the one and only! Then when you're clear on that, I think there'll be nothing stopping you. What you could do is team up with somebody to hang out with some other girls. If after this you still reckon Anna is the one, you will not be playing with other girls anymore; that's it." Fabio looked as if he was onto something fabulous. Matt was a bit hesitant, but secretly liking the idea as he was in need of some physical rewards.

"Your ideas have worked so far, so why not? I know a guy who seems to hang out with a lot of different girls—Ben from upstairs."

As Matt mentioned the name 'Ben,' Fabio's expression changed immediately. "Oh no, you can't be serious? You mean Ben the graphic designer, that guy is a galah[39] and..."

Matt cut him off. "I know, I know. You don't like him because he is arrogant. He is so metrosexual that the girls love hanging with him because they think they are safe, which they of course aren't at all! But surely

---

[39] A 'galah' is a silly person. The expression comes from an Aussie bird of the same name because of its antics and the noise it makes.

he could make me more popular and could introduce me to some girls." Matt put on his puppy dog face (he'd learnt from his two pups, Mickey and Minnie) to convince Fabio.

"You do whatever you need to do, but remember this: Aligning with the right person can work wonders and aligning with the wrong person can be very damaging to your name and personal brand." Fabio still looked a bit concerned but happy to see his student ready to take action immediately.

Ben was a real ladies' man who worked hard and played hard. To most people in the company, he was friendly despite being a bit arrogant. The girls loved him for his metrosexual, city boy/ad agency style. No one knew much about him. He kept his personal life very secret except for the fact that he went out partying almost every night.

The next morning, Matt had to brief the design studio on a job, so he took the opportunity to strike up a conversation with Ben. "Hey, Ben, how's things?"

Ben immediately cut to the chase. "Mate, I know you don't usually talk to me, so what's up?"

To his surprise, Matt found himself spilling the beans and telling Ben about Anna in every detail. Ben took pity and decided to take Matt under his wing. Matt felt a bit concerned later about the way metrosexual Ben had made him feel safe enough to open up. He just couldn't help it! Little did he know that it would later bite him in the bum.

Sure enough, the two of them agreed to meet up after work and head to a bar where Ben was planning to meet up with some girls. They had a relatively uneventful night but enjoyed the company, so Ben suggested they go out again the following day and both bring some girls along. Matt thought things were really looking up now!

By now you know that nurturing relationships and collaboration with other business owners is paramount. In this chapter we will look at three different ways to use the power of partnerships and how to make them beneficial for everyone involved: strategic alliances, referral systems and sponsorships. These strategies are some of the fastest ways to market and grow a small business.

Strategic alliance

Forming strategic alliances (also known as joint ventures) is one of our favourite marketing strategies. The name sounds much more scary or complex than it really is. It is basically teaming up with a business or organisation that is non-competitive but has the same target market and already has a big list of loyal contacts.

The trick is to find a business or organisation that has the **same target market** as you and is **not in competition** with you. You then **offer extra value** to their target market and this makes their business look good in the process. This strategy can help you generate a huge amount of clients with a small amount of effort on your behalf, once set up. And it also works well even if you do not have a huge database yet.

As Fabio discussed earlier, the key is to **find the right business**. Not an easy task. So make sure you select carefully. We always encourage business owners in our community to work together (rather than against each other). Let's illustrate this with a few successful examples of some of our clients:

- Karla, a nutritionist, has formed a strategic alliance with a gym. They are both targeting people who want to make some changes in their life. The gym is focusing on fitness, the nutritionist on the food. Karla offers the gym vouchers for free nutritional assessments that the gym uses as an incentive to sign up more members. It's a win-win situation as the gym looks good and offers a bonus to new members, and Karla gets great exposure, knowing that her free assessments will lead to more paid work if she does a great job. Plus because the gym's clients already have trust in the gym, Karla gains instant trust from being endorsed by the gym. Let's call this trust, 'osmosis,' to sound cool. It works wonderfully!

- Roger, a graphic designer, partnered with a business coach and offered a free logo design for the business coach's clients. When the clients who took up the offer needed more design work done, they turned to Roger, given that he had done a fabulous job on their free logo and they liked his work.

- Will, a coffee shop owner, has partnered with the local news agency, and every customer who spends over $20 in the news agency receives a voucher for a free coffee. This increases the average amount spent in the news agency, and when the customers come into Will's coffee shop for a coffee, they often buy something else. And better yet, because the coffee is delicious and customer service great, Will wins over additional regular customers.

- Lisa, a chiropractor, teamed up with Renate, the owner of a children's play centre, by offering free health checks for busy mums and their kids at the play centre. A lot of the mums loved Lisa's service and booked in for more sessions at her practice. Renate's play centre is considered one of the best places for mums and kids to hang out due to partnering with people like Lisa and offering amazing services. A winner for all involved.

- A photographer, a life coach and a gym owner met at a workshop, got together and worked out how they can help grow each other's databases. They organised a competition where the three winners received a glamorous photo-shoot, free membership at the gym and free life coaching sessions. By promoting the competition through all of their databases, social media networks and at the gym and studio, all of them gained more exposure to new people. This case was a Win-Win-Win.

If your potential strategic alliance partner does not know your products or services, offer them for free so they can test them and talk about how good you and your offerings are when recommending you to their clients. No one can recommend something they have not tried.

Are you ready to set up your own strategic alliance? It's pretty easy; you just need to think a little bit outside the box.

Here are some questions that will help you get started in planning your joint ventures:

- What type of clients would you like to attract? Who are you targeting?
- What other non-competing businesses provide services to them?
- Does the business have a great attitude and values you can align yourself with without damaging your brand?
- Are their clients likely to want to spend money with you?
- What are you going to offer? The offer needs to be perceived as valuable or the potential strategic

alliance partner won't be interested. You want the agreement to be a win-win situation for both parties involved.

- How are you going to communicate your offer to the potential partner (email, phone call, letter, in person)? Following up in person definitely helps.
- How will you present your offer to their clients (vouchers, flyers, cards, posters, banners etc.)?
- How much time and money will it take you to set up? How much more business would you need to cover the costs?
- How can you make this relationship mutually beneficial?

Before pitching your idea to a business that you want to align with, **put the strategy in writing** so that you are prepared with a realistic plan that is mutually beneficial. Always put yourself into the shoes of your potential partner and think *'Would I like this if I was him/her?'* Your offer should be perceived as a bonus organised by the partner business. For example *"As a valued client of Johnny's you are entitled to a free oil check at Peter's Car Shed."* This way Johnny's looks generous and Peter's Car Shed has gained instant trust as it is being recommended by Johnny's.

It is smart to offer to pay for any expenses like flyers or vouchers that you will use for the campaign. Also, offer to write any correspondence your alliance partner can use, such as emails and letters, to let their clients know about the special 'gift.' This way it's all done for them and 'being too busy' is no excuse. Make it as easy as possible for them.

We think you are ready to get started! Get creative; there are lots of opportunities just around the corner.

It's your turn to take action

1. Find the right business (or businesses) to work with.
2. Come up with a plan of how this partnership could work. Remember, it must be beneficial for the partner's business, not just yours.
3. Contact the business either via phone or email, and try to meet with the decision maker to discuss your proposal. Please note: Never try to steal another business's clients. Your goal is to offer extra value and make your strategic partner look like a legend in the process. Always think about how you can help them and they will help you.
4. Once you've reached an agreement with your strategic partner, create promotional materials you both can use to promote this relationship. Make it as easy as possible for the other business. Even if all they need is an email to their database, offer to write it for them.
5. Nurture the relationship with your partner and think about how you can make it even better.

Referral system

Unfortunately, Matt's strategic alliance didn't go very well. He should have selected his partner more carefully. As he had promised Ben that he would bring some girls along on Friday after work, he finally ended up calling Anna and inviting her to go out with them. He didn't know who else to call, and he also didn't want to tell Ben that he didn't know any other girls to bring. So, Anna was pretty much the only option (so much for playing the field a bit more). He would find himself later wishing that he had never asked her to join them; a date would have been so much more appropriate.

Anna was happy to join them for a bit and brought two of her girlfriends as well. It didn't take Matt very long to work out that he had made a huge mistake. Firstly, how was he going to meet new girls if Anna was there? Secondly, he realised he didn't want to meet new girls anyway as all he cared about was Anna. And thirdly, Ben was living up to his reputation and had started sleazing onto Anna straight away. Matt felt a bit left out and decided to get Anna's attention by buying her a fancy cocktail. There was a big line at the bar, and when Matt returned both Ben and Anna were gone. He was standing in the middle of the bar, a fancy cocktail in each hand, and no Anna anywhere. He felt like the biggest loser and feared the worst. He asked Anna's girlfriends but they hadn't seen her either. To drown his sorrows, he drank both cocktails in the space of fifteen minutes and then went home.

Matt spent the rest of the weekend kicking himself and stressing over what had happened with Ben and Anna. He hated himself for not listening to Fabio and finding a good strategic alliance partner. I shouldn't have trusted Ben.

On Sunday afternoon, he finally cracked and nervously called Anna. His palms were sweaty and he could feel his heart thumping like a sledge hammer in his chest as she picked up. "Hi Matt," she said, sounding a bit distracted.

"How did you enjoy your night on Friday?" he asked. "Yeah, it was okay." Anna sounded rushed. "Listen Matt, I gotta split. I'm looking after my two nieces today. I'll speak to you later."

I'll speak to you later? What does that mean? Matt was disappointed. Was she with that bastard Ben?

He picked up the phone again and this time dialed Fabio's number as he needed a confidence booster from Cupid. "Oh God, did I tell you or not?" Fabio obviously wasn't surprised at all. "Okay, I didn't want to pull this card until a real emergency hit, but I think this just might be the time! Now, listen mate... carefully..." Fabio was now whispering into his phone, making sure his wife couldn't hear him. "Things are obviously not going well with Anna, right? Why don't you keep looking a bit more? I've got a friend, Daisy, who works at the Silo Bar in town. She owes me a favour. She knows lots of girls that might be able to give you some 'pain relief.' Let me give her a call and ask her if she could hook you up."

"What are you talking about? I'm not that desperate! And I can certainly meet a girl without a 'referral' from Daisy..." But after an awkward silence,

Matt added "Bugger it! Where is that Silo Bar, anyway?" Matt got up from his armchair and started walking to the door to put his shoes on.

"It's not what you think it is, Matt. What I mean is, she knows a lot of lovely girls and could introduce you to someone if you care for some Sunday night company."

At the Silo bar, Daisy introduced Matt to a group of girls straight away. Daisy was serving them all champagnes to toast on friendship. One of the girls caught Matt's attention; her name was Katie. He couldn't put his finger on it, but somehow she seemed very familiar; he felt like he'd met her before. They started chatting, and even though he couldn't get Anna off his mind, he asked Katie out for a casual dinner on Wednesday night. He figured it would be nice to have some nice female company.

Having great referral partners in your business is invaluable as referral business is one of the best sources of new leads. Referrals usually come with a recommendation to use your services, which means that they are already pre-sold.

If you belong to a networking group, you might be familiar with the term 'referral partner.' In certain networking groups, such as BNI[40], it's common to

---

[40] BNI stands for Business Networking International and is the world's largest business referral organisation that has networking chapters in over 40 countries. The purpose of

give each other referrals to help grow each member's business.

You do not have to belong to a networking group to find referral partners. There is a range of different ways to find suitable referral partners. Here are a couple:

Find a complementary business

As discussed above, find someone who offers a complementary service and suggest you both refer clients to each other. For example, if you are a web developer, you might want to refer business to a graphic designer and vice-versa. If you are an accountant, you might be able to refer business to a bookkeeper and vice-versa. If you own a hotel, you might refer business to a local restaurant and vice versa. If you are a builder, you might refer business to a tiler. We're sure you've got the point. It really is just a matter of finding someone you could help out by referring business, and they could refer people to you. Again, make it beneficial for them; it has to be a two-way street.

---

being part of a group such as BNI is to give and receive referrals.

Leverage your own contacts

Your happy clients are your best referral partners. If your clients are happy with your services or products, they would surely refer you to their friends. Or would they? Yes, they would, but you have to ask them. Some people are natural 'connecters,' but most people, even though they love you and mean well, just forget about sending business your way.

In order to make it easier for them to refer business your way, give them a good reason to do so. For example, give your happy clients a gift voucher for your product that they can pass on to a friend. This way they also get to help out a friend who might need your products or services.

The other way to make it easier for them to think about referring you is if you reward them for their referrals. Maybe you can give them a voucher for a dinner at the local restaurant or a bottle of wine for every customer they send your way.

Susie, a massage therapist who did not know much about marketing, organised a letterbox drop that did not work at all. For $1,400 in expenses she got one new customer through the door (and she didn't even want to work with the guy because he was sleazy!). Ouch!

When she came to us with her marketing problems, we decided to implement a referral strategy where each of her customers got two gift cards to give to friends for a thirty minute free massage. She got a lot of new potential customers through the door and most of them upgraded to a one hour massage, so she still made a bit of money. But what's more important, because she provided an excellent service, she managed to grow her regular client base in the process at no cost (except for her time spent during the first time they came in).

> ### It's your turn to take action
>
> This one is very easy to set up, so why not get onto it straight away? Just think about an irresistible offer you could give your prospects that will not ruin you. Then create some beautiful gift cards or special deal cards and give them to your happy clients to pass on. Only give your client one or two cards to pass on, otherwise the perceived value will go down and the card is suddenly not so special anymore.

Sponsorships

As Matt was chatting away with Katie, he thought she was pretty cool, but more in a 'mates' kind of way. She told him that she was working in a not-for-profit organisation that sponsors children in the Third World to enable them to go to school. She shared that a lot of the bigger companies were really keen to be seen as a supporter of their charity, though in most cases it was not so much to help the kids but more to look like 'good guys.'

"The kids are so grateful. Only $400 a year enables a primary school kid to go to school and get a proper education." Katie explained enthusiastically.

Matt suddenly pulled out his credit card. "I'd love to support a child," he said.

Katie's blue eyes widened in surprise, and then she cracked up laughing. "I wasn't giving you a sales pitch right now, was I? You don't have to do this Matt, although it would be much appreciated."

"I'm serious. I really want to help. By the way, it looks like Daisy is paying for the champagne, and that would have cost me half of the fee." Matt started feeling better in Katie's company.

"Well, that's true. I can't take your credit card here, though. But I'll send you a form to fill in tomorrow when I'm back at work. Thank you for being so generous!"

As Matt was lying in bed that night he was thinking that if he didn't end up with a girlfriend, at least he would become a better person in the process. Firstly, he had adopted two orphan puppies, and now he was going to help kids in the Third World! He was planning on asking some of his corporate advertising clients whether they would like to support Katie's charity too. They could all make a huge difference—and improve their brand image in the process. And with that thought, he fell fast asleep.

For some businesses, sponsoring events, clubs or people works really well to get exposure and to make a big difference at the same time.

The same rule applies as in your strategic alliance strategy discussed above. **Find a club or events to sponsor that have the same target market you do**. For example, if you work with corporates, it doesn't make sense to sponsor family events. Rather, look at approaching golfing clubs or corporate events—wherever you will find your market hanging out.

Likewise, if your target market is families or children, look at sponsoring schools, sports clubs, fundraisers, and so on. There is no lack of opportunities!

You can offer your support in different ways. You don't always have to donate money when it comes to sponsorships. You could also look at donating branded clothing, your services or products for free, speaking at their events for free, or donating raffle prizes or small gifts for goodie bags at fundraising events.

What are the benefits for you besides looking like the good guy and feeling great? Depending on your sponsorship, the club or person you are sponsoring can give you: access to their clients by sending your marketing materials to their clients; an email or newsletter to their database; your flyers in their foyer; your logo and a mention on their website; your pull-up banner displayed at their events and so on. The opportunities are endless.

One of our clients, Sandro, who is an optometrist, loves supporting the local community. His target market is families, so he is regularly supporting schools and local sporting teams. In return he gets great exposure in their newsletters, on their websites and at their events.

We believe very much in combining business and philanthropy to make a difference through social business. One of our projects is called **Bananas for Everyone** where we are financially supporting a school in South Africa. A few of our clients have joined in the effort and are donating money, their products or services.

Everyone can make a difference, no matter how big or small!

It's your turn to take action

1. Choose your favourite charity, school, event or project that you would like to support, and make it happen!
2. Let your clients know that you are supporting a certain cause. Some might even want to join in the effort.

14

Copywriting that captivates

Ooh... You've got such a way with words

"I'm an artist; the alphabet is my palette."

~ CHRISTO HALL

ON MONDAY MORNING, MATT WAS IN DESPERATE need of some 'Fabio Fab Advice.' So, he booked himself in for a 'very important meeting' through the agency diary.

"This must be serious," Fabio smiled as he met Matt in a meeting room. Matt was fired up. He told Fabio again about his weekend and how he still couldn't stop thinking about Anna and that he might have messed it all up.

"Calm down, Matt." Fabio's voice was soothing like that of a master yogi. "There are plenty of ways to get Anna back, and there will always be competition. As long as you always do your best, and stay true to your values, things will work out."

"I really want Anna back. I've still got the phone numbers for other girls I met at the singles party, and I'm meeting Katie for dinner on Wednesday. But all I want is Anna. By the way, do you know anyone (not Ben!) who might want to go out with me and Katie Wednesday night? Katie is bringing her sister along because she promised to hang out with her, so I thought I might bring a mate. It's just a friendly dinner."

"Mate, you go and enjoy the dinner with Katie and her sister, and try to take your mind off Anna for a while. That's my only advice to you at the moment; you need to chill. And no, I don't know anyone. Just consider yourself lucky that you have two girls to take out, not one!"

"Katie's cool," Matt said. "She seems so familiar but I don't think I could ever fall in love with her. I'm gonna do some free copywriting to help her encourage more young people to sponsor her charity. That will take my mind off Anna."

"You know Matt, men are like dogs and women are like cats..." Fabio went on and on about the nature of men and women... Meanwhile, Matt's thoughts were wandering and he missed a lot of it. He realised that he still had a bit to learn; it seemed like a never-ending journey to him. *I guess life is a continual learning curve* he thought as he partly listened to Fabio saying something about cats being impossible to read and hard to tame whereas dogs could be read like a book...

There is one marketing skill that is unfortunately often neglected in small business—and that is copywriting[41]. Yet copywriting is one of the most important marketing skills of a small business owner. Why? Because the words that you use to market your business are crucial; they will absolutely determine the success of your marketing strategies and materials. Even a simple change in your headline can immediately change your results. **Great copy will grab the attention of your target market and inspire the reader to take a certain action**, whether it is to give you a call, go to your website or test-drive your product or service.

If you are like most small business owners, you probably don't enjoy writing and would rather outsource to an expert. However, it is really hard to find a good copywriter, and besides that, it's good to have a basic knowledge of copywriting. It is one of the most sought after and least talked about skills in the world of business. It's no surprise that the best copywriters charge thousands of

---

[41] Copywriting is a common word in marketing and advertising and means the use of words to promote something. Or in short, copywriting = text.

dollars for a single document. If you do find a good copywriter and can afford his or her services, it's a good investment considering the massive difference a well-written marketing piece can make in terms of response rates and increased sales.

The reality for most small business owners is they don't have thousands of dollars to invest initially; so in this chapter we'll give you some tips and tricks to make your copy work for you. Use this chapter as a reference guide for writing some new marketing materials or revamping your old ones. A little side note here—**please do not expect your graphic designers to write the copy for you**. Their job is to make your stuff look good, not to write copy for you.

Research, research, research...

This is probably the most important lesson in this chapter: really understanding your target market by researching them.

Before you start writing any copy, you need to first do your research. And this is where most people go wrong. They just start writing away without really understanding their target market, writing about themselves: **my** product, **my** qualifications, **my** family, **my** cats, **my** new car. Okay, that might be a bit exaggerated, but you get the idea. Unless you are a celebrity and people want to know everything about you and your life, no one will care.

Once you have determined your target market (or target markets), you need to conduct some research to really understand them—**their** interests, **their** needs, **their** wants, **their** frustrations. Why? So that you can write marketing materials that speak to their **heart**, which means understanding them so much that they will go 'ah this guy or girl really gets me.' This is what will give you an advantage over your competitors.

In his book *My Life in Advertising*, Claude C. Hopkins[42] states that 'people in general could never be judged by ourselves' and continues to say 'I know of nothing more ridiculous than grey-haired boards of directors deciding on what housewives want.' He is not saying that grey-haired directors don't know anything about housewives, but he is talking about the importance of finding out from your target market what they want and need, rather than making assumptions from the board room. Why not get amongst your target market and ask people about their opinion as they purchase your products and services?

---

[42] Claude C. Hopkins was one of the first advertising guys to use marketing principles that are still extremely successful today. *My Life in Advertising* has become a marketing classic for professional modern-day copywriters.

Every target market has their own 'language' that you need to tap into to gain their attention. A retiree would 'speak' differently to a university student and have completely different interests. When you are travelling in a foreign country, you don't really pay attention to the ads in the local paper because they do not 'speak' your language, right? (Unless you know their language, of course). You do not want that to happen to your marketing material and adverts.

The fact is people buy from people they know, like and trust. If you can describe your ideal clients' problems or desires better than they can themselves, you can 'speak' in their language and they will feel like you understand and know them; you will build instant trust. **If you have a deeper understanding of your prospects than your competitors do, you will be their obvious choice every time. Guaranteed!**

Okay, you are ready to do your own research. (And by the way, researching is half your job done!) **So how can you research your target market?**

There are a few different, easy methods to get you started:

Talk to people

Communicate with people and find out what they want more than anything in regards to your products or services. Asking questions and communicating with your prospects, clients, friends or family is one of the best ways to receive valuable information. And who knows, maybe one of your friends just happens to have the million dollar idea or insight!

Survey your clients (and prospects)

Set up a short survey in www.surveymonkey.com, a free online survey tool, asking such questions as:

- *How does my product or service benefit you?*
- *What would make it even better?*
- *What is one thing we could do to improve our services?*

Once you have got the questions set up, you can send the survey link to your database, post it on your social media networks and ask people to help you out. This way you can provide them with an even more amazing product or service. Clients love having a say and feeling as though they can influence your decisions to their benefit. So make them a part of it.

Google

Google is your best friend. Use Google to research what your competitors are doing and also what your prospects are looking for. The *Google Keyword*

Planner[43] will help you find out what keywords your prospects are searching for online.

What is your intention?

Before writing copy for an article, advertisement, your website, a flyer or any marketing material, think about your intention. What do you want your copy to do? What is your intention? What action do you want the reader to take? Do you want the reader to pick up the phone and call? To hold onto your flyer because it's of value? To opt in on your website? To be educated about something? To build trust?

If you don't know what your intention is and you clearly communicate that to your prospects, then they most likely will not know what to do either.

Headlines

The goal of your headline is to capture your readers' attention as quickly as possible. Think of your writing like stepping stones—the first sentence should engage the reader and lead them to the second and so on.

Your headline is usually what engages your readers and makes them stop and read.

---

[43] Check out *Chapter 10 More Online Marketing Strategies* for more information about how to use the Google Keyword Planner.

The late David Ogilvy, who is also called 'the father of advertising,' said: 'On the average, five times as many people read the headline as read the body copy. When you have written your headline, you have spent eighty cents out of your dollar.'[44]

Create headlines that define a need that your prospects have.

For example:
- *Discover how you can lose weight without starving yourself.* The need here is losing weight.
- *Double your sales in 30 days without ever cold calling again.* The need here is more sales.

Mentioning your ideal client in the headline is another way of capturing their attention.

For example:
- *Attention Home Owners. Do you feel like you are paying too much for your mortgage?*
- *Are you a business owner and tired of paying too much on your tax bill?*

Once you have caught the interest of the reader through your headline, they will continue reading.

As mentioned earlier, a change in your headline can have a huge impact on your return, so the best thing is to test and measure your headlines. Compare these two headlines for example:
- *Buy advertising for your business!*
- *Discover how to increase your sales instantly.*

---

[44] www.brainyquote.com.

Both have the same objective (to sell advertising), but the second one will make the reader more curious and more likely to keep reading. Just as with all of your marketing, aim to add value rather than to ask for money.

Numbers in the headline work well, such as:

- *The 5 Biggest Mistakes...*
- *The 7 Keys to...*
- *3 Things You Need to Know...*

After catching your prospects' attention with your headline, you want to build up a need for your product or service. This can be done by either **focusing on their frustrations or their desires**. Let us give you a quick example. If you sell a weight-loss product or service, you can either focus on the pain by talking about how frustrating it is to not fit into your favourite jeans and feeling tired and unmotivated. Or you can focus on the desires by talking about the pleasures of feeling sexy, energised, motivated and happy being at their desired weight.

Always make your prospects feel like you know and understand their problems and desires; hence, all the research you did in the first place!

Adding some facts and figures is great too. For example: *'Did you know that 95% of all diets don't work?'*

And remember to keep your focus on them, not on yourself. You can worry about yourself later, maybe over a beer or glass of wine with your best friend. If you flick through some marketing material, you will soon realise that a lot of advertisements mainly speak about how good a product or service is rather than focusing on the prospect—not very effective.

You only mention yourself and your solution after you have built up a need for what you've got.

So the formula to create kick-butt copy is the following:

1. Get to know your ideal client and find out what their needs are that your solution can meet.
2. Capture their attention with a great headline.
3. Build up a need for your product or service by speaking about their deepest frustrations and desires.
4. Then offer the solution and the next steps for them to take. This is your Call to Action.

Keep it real, man

Keeping your writing **conversational**, as if you are talking to one person, will make it more engaging for your readers. You can achieve this conversational tone easily by giving your prospect a name and writing with that person in mind.

Joe Vitale, the author of *Hypnotic Writing*, goes as far as to recommend writing with your computer screen turned off so you can just let the writing flow without stopping and overthinking. You then edit later.

You want people to resonate with your character, so allow your personality to shine through. Too much copy out there is without any personality and is just plain boring to read. Make your copy stand out by being authentic and interesting.

Use words that paint a positive image in your reader's mind. The human mind is a genius, and one single word can paint a whole picture. So look over your writing very closely and think of what comes to mind. Sometimes it helps to ask someone else to look over your copy, preferably someone in your target market.

Guaranteed

If you believe in your product or service, then why not offer a guarantee? It will instantly increase your sales, no doubt! Yes, it can be scary thinking that someone might ask for their money back; but if you offer a great service then you have nothing to worry about. We offer a money-back guarantee on our programs at Basic Bananas, and no one has ever asked for their money back. What the guarantee also does is hold us accountable to always deliver the best possible service.

The most effective guarantees are tangible. For example, if you were buying a product for $100 and the guarantee stated 'We guarantee you will be 100% satisfied or we'll give you $110 back,' you would think they are either pretty confident in their product or they are crazy. Either way, there's less risk to buy from them.

So, offer a guarantee and make it known by placing it on all of your marketing materials. Anything that lowers the risk of making a mistake when buying your product or service needs to be made public.

A basic formula is 'We guarantee you will be 100% satisfied or we give you <insert guarantee here>.' Simple.

Pain or pleasure?

World famous author and motivational speaker, Anthony Robbins, teaches that people will do more to avoid pain than they will to experience pleasure. So, sometimes you might need to make people aware of the pain that they are experiencing, or will be experiencing, if they don't make a change (the desired change involving your product or service, of course).

We also like focusing on the pleasures something is giving us as it is positive, and some people (including us!) are more pleasure-oriented and driven. So some will prefer to read about the pleasures your product or service offers.

In your copy, then, you can either **focus on the problems and frustrations** your target market is experiencing and how your product solves them, or you can **focus on the pleasure** your product or service will bring to the user. Depending on your target market and product or service, one of them will work a bit better than the other. It's best to try both approaches and test and measure your success.

A quick example to illustrate both tactics:

As mentioned earlier, a weight loss expert could either write about the pain and frustrations such as *'Are you tired of being overweight? Are you over not having the energy to play with your kids?'* Or he could write about the pleasure and desires such as *'Are you ready for the body of your dreams? Imagine feeling good and confident every day.'*

One of our clients, Anita, the owner of a cleaning business, used both approaches: 'Did you know that 80% of people get sick because of dirty carpets? Are you fed up with a dirty house holding you back from living the life of your dreams? Are you embarrassed to have visitors?' Her pleasure-focused statement: 'The 7 benefits of having a clean house. Impress your visitors with a beautifully clean house.'

The second approach focusing on pleasure seems a bit nicer, but sometimes people just need a bit of a reality-check and a poke in the ribs (or kick up the bum) to take action. Both approaches worked well for Anita.

There's only one left? i've got to have it...

Whenever something is rare, people want it much more than if there is a lot of it—it's just human nature. If we think something will be running out of stock, we really do not want to miss out, even though we might not need that thing right now.

Let's look at a practical example. If you are interested in buying a pair of jeans and there are only two pairs remaining in your size before they are discontinued, then you feel you better make a decision pretty quickly and buy them right now. Otherwise, someone else might get them, right? Nobody wants to feel like they are missing out.

It's called the **law of scarcity** or **the** rule of the few, as Dr. Cialdini calls it. He states:

> "Opportunities seem more valuable to us when their availability is limited. The idea of potential loss plays a large role in human decision making. In fact, people seem to be more motivated by the thought of losing something than by the thought of gaining something of equal value. For instance, homeowners told how much money they could lose from inadequate insulation are more likely to insulate their homes than those told how much money they could save."

Cialdini's research agrees with Anthony Robbins' **pain versus pleasure principle** above. It is easier for people to take action to move away from pain and avoid the fear of loss.

Including **limited numbers available** in your marketing materials is very effective—but only if you are authentic and not just abusing this principle. If it's not true, do not say it. People are not stupid and will find out pretty quickly whether you are an ethical marketer or not.

If you say there's a certain amount of something left, then make it real and stick to it. For example, if you say *'the first 5 people to buy <your product or service> will get 50% off,'* then stick to it and only give it to the first five people, even if ten people call up for the promotion. It's all about being authentic and ethical, and not tricking your prospects.

The clock's ticking...

Now consider this. If the two pairs of jeans remaining were also on sale for a 30% discount for 'today only,' suddenly the risk of missing out on the discount comes into play as well.

We call this **the law of urgency**, which means that whenever there is a bit of urgency to take action, more people will take that action so they do not miss out on a good deal. Urgency helps a prospect make a decision faster because if they wait any longer they might miss out. The fear of potential loss comes into play again.

Imagine if you are thinking about buying that pair of jeans and they are on special until tomorrow. You are more likely to jump onto it, rather than wait and see, because you do not want to miss out.

Shops and supermarkets use the principle of urgency and scarcity really well to move stock. Discounted products in a supermarket will sell much faster than the ones that are not discounted. People tend to buy ten blocks of discounted chocolate, stocking up on it because they were half price, even though they never intended to buy any chocolate.

Again, it goes without saying that you use this principle with integrity and not to trick somebody into buying your product or service. If you have a special offer until Sunday, make sure that special offer is only valid until Sunday. Unfortunately, there are quite a few marketers out there that completely abuse that principle and they promise a '24-hour quick sale,' and two days later when you check back in, the 24-hour sale is still there. Not cool. Their credibility and trust is instantly gone.

If everyone's doing it, it *must* be good...

It's a lovely Friday night and you are taking your partner out for dinner. There are two great restaurants next to each other; one is full of people, the other one is almost empty. Which one do you choose? If you are like most human beings, you would pick the one with lots of people in it because 'it must be good.' The principle of **social proof** is extremely effective for small businesses. If the empty restaurant got a few friends to just sit at the tables, more people would come in, guaranteed.

We've tested this principle, combined with urgency, at a friend's market stall. Her stall was not attracting a lot of people, so we got a few friends to admire her goods. In only a matter of minutes, passers-by had stopped, interested in her goods. 'It must be good' if there are so many people looking. We took the experiment one step further, and when a lady was looking at a cute denim jacket, one of the market stall owner's friends looked at it as well and told her how awesome it is and whether she's got another one. Sure enough, the slightly interested lady turned from interested to committed and asked our friend to put it aside for her while she went to the ATM[45]. She even left her wallet behind to make sure the jacket did not get sold to the other potential

---

[45] ATM does not mean Always Totally Motivated. It stands for Automatic Teller Machine. It's where you get money out with your card.

buyer. The fear of loss made her take action faster. Interesting!

A few night clubs are using, or should we say abusing, this principle really well by making sure that in front of the club there is always a long line of people waiting to get in, even though the club is actually almost empty. Having a line outside gives the impression that it must be a very popular place to go to.

According to Cialdini, 'In general, when we are unsure of ourselves, when the situation is unclear or ambiguous, when uncertainty reigns, we are most likely to look to and accept the actions of others as correct.' He also talks about how advertisers love to inform us about the 'fastest-growing' and 'best-selling' or 'most wanted' products and services because they do not have to convince the target market that the product or service is good. They merely need to say that many other people think so—social proof.

The most common and fastest way to gain social proof for small businesses is in the form of **happy client testimonials**.

If you can show your prospects that lots of people are using your product and are happy with the results, then more than likely they will be less afraid of buying from you.

Great testimonials are the ones that overcome objections your prospects might have. For example, if the main objection people have when considering buying from you is that your product or service is too expensive, a fantastic testimonial would be something like this:

> 'I wasn't sure about using a <financial planner> because of the cost, but as it turned out I have saved so much more money that I would have missed out on otherwise. The value I have received is priceless. I would recommend <Freddy Financial> to anyone looking to save money and gain a huge return on their dollars invested.'

It goes without saying that you don't fake your testimonials! Only use real, authentic ones. To make your testimonial even more effective, include a photograph and more details about the person who wrote it (with their permission of course). On your website, **video testimonials** are fabulous too.

So, when writing your marketing copy, think about how you can integrate the laws of urgency, scarcity and social proof and you'll see the difference!

You want a deal?

Let's look at these laws in action! Online 'deals'[46] became so popular and there were different companies popping up all the time trying to get a

---

[46] Please do not advertise your business on one of these sites unless you have a strategic plan in place to upsell or gain regular clients. They can be very dangerous and a lot of businesses paid out of pocket for such online campaigns and were never able to make up for the loss.

piece of the action. The bigger players like cudo.com.au, livingsocial.com, spreetz.com.au and ouffer.com turned over millions of dollars. When you look a little closer, it's no surprise why.

They access all of the principles of marketing discussed above:

- They have a good deal, providing a lot of value.
- They have a limited time. On some sites a timer is actually counting down on the page (urgency).
- They often have limited numbers (scarcity).
- They show how many other people have bought the offer so far (social proof).

They are the perfect model to make people take action fast, and the results show. (Whether they are actually good for the participating business is a huge other topic and it depends on the business).

Ebay is another example that illustrates the use of the marketing principles we have discussed so far: There is **urgency** as the clock counts down, **scarcity** in limited numbers and **social proof** comes from the other bidders all wanting the same product and from the ratings of products and sellers.

If you visited a shop that had a sign saying *'50% off all stock TODAY ONLY'* you would most likely want to have a good look around and get busy buying the things you want but do not need. You probably would not have entered the shop in the first place, but the fear of missing out on a special deal made you go in. The reason post-Christmas sales work so well in shops is because we know they are for a limited time and there is limited stock available.

In a lot of cases, if people can wait until they are ready to make a decision, they might not choose your product when they are finally ready, or they will just take forever to make up their mind. But if you have a sale on and there is only four of a particular item left or four minutes until the offer closes, then people will pay attention.

Why does this stuff work? Because **opportunities seem more valuable to us when their availability is limited.**

Tell them what to do

One of the most important (yet most forgotten) parts of your marketing materials is your **Call to Action**. Simply tell the reader exactly what to do next. For example:

- *Call 1300 691 883 now for your free check-up.*
- *Go to www.example.com for your free guide.*

Make it simple. People need to know exactly what to do next. If you can read your Call to Action to a 3-year-old child and she understands what to do next, then you have done well. If she is a little unsure about what to do, then you better review it.

It's your turn to take action

Take these steps to create effective copy:

1. Research your core target market's needs and wants. ASK them.
2. Set your intention for the copy.
3. Create headlines that define needs
4. Write in the target market's language, directly addressing their core needs.
5. Write in a conversational tone and focus on the positive.
6. Offer a guarantee.
7. Use pain-focused or pleasure-focused questions.
8. Utilise the laws of urgency, scarcity and social proof.
9. Utilise the laws of urgency, scarcity and social proof.

Finish with a simple Call to Action.

15

Advertisements

Handsome man looking for
handsome woman

*"Nobody reads ads. People read what interests them.
Sometimes it's an ad."*

~ HOWARD GOSSAGE

IT WAS WEDNESDAY NIGHT AND MATT WAS LOOKING forward to a quiet dinner with Katie, the charity girl he met at the bar on Sunday night, and her sister. They had decided to go for sushi. He didn't know any other guy to invite so it was just him.

Matt arrived a couple of minutes early, so he ordered a bottle of sake and three cups. As he was thinking about his life and how much he'd learnt over the past few weeks, Katie arrived. "'My sister is running a few minutes late, but she said not to wait for her."

Matt really liked Katie and thought she could become a good friend, but he couldn't stop thinking about Anna. About twenty minutes later, as they were happily chatting away and toasting to their friendship with sake, Anna walked into the restaurant and started heading straight for their table. "What are you doing here?" Anna said in disbelief.

Matt stuttered, "Ahh, um... What are you doing here?"

Anna's disbelief quickly turned into anger. "I was supposed to have dinner with my sister and some loser! What sort of tricks are you up to? How do you know my sister? Trying to get to my sister, you loser. And you just left me alone at the pub with Ben so he could open his flood gates of BS[47]. I had to run off because it was the only way to get rid of him. Why do I always seem to attract shitty guys like you? What are you doing here with my sister, seriously?" Only then did Anna pause for breath.

Matt's panic levels went through the roof. He felt like he was having an asthma attack and could hardly get any words out. "Oh no, no. This is a huge misunderstanding..." Matt started to explain the situation, but Anna turned on her heels and walked out of the restaurant quicker than a possum[48] up a tree.

---

[47] BS: Bull***t.
[48] A possum is a cute native Australian animal that belongs to the marsupial species. It looks like an Aussie version of a squirrel.

Two weeks went by and Matt didn't hear a word from Anna despite his many voice messages on her phone—and a few to Katie begging for her help.

Fabio, feeling sorry for Matt, suggested he write an ad for Anna using the copywriting skills he taught him earlier. "Let's get creative, Matt! Didn't you tell me Anna reads the local paper every day on her way to work? I know the editor of that paper, and I'll get him to place your ad in it." Fabio smiled a smile that could melt a snowman in Alaska.

"What am I going to say, Fabio? I don't want her to think that I'm chasing other girls anymore! I'm only interested in her!" Matt's voice sounded desperate.

"No, mate. This time we are targeting her and her only! Yes, other girls might read it, but the ad will only speak to Anna. She will see it and realise that you are speaking to her and really mean it. Just imagine a very cheesy scene in a Bollywood flick." Fabio started drifting off into dreamland and was about to describe the movie scene he was seeing, but Matt was already onto it and started writing... the clock was ticking.

It took Matt only about eight minutes to come up with his ad to get Anna back.

Help!
Advertising guy looking for his heart that got stolen by a girl.
There is one suspect.
If
your name is Anna and

> you are a fashion designer who was supposed to have sushi with her sister and a loser, then it's you...
> Please call Matt NOW on 0428 xxx xxx to book in for a three-course meal at your favourite restaurant for free.

First up, **advertisements are not your best marketing strategy for most businesses.** We are including this chapter because a lot of small businesses do pay (too much!) for advertisements, and if you choose this route we want to make sure that you maximise your investment. Running ads in a paper is even sometimes the only marketing activity some businesses use. But by now you know so many other effective marketing strategies that you might choose to ditch this one unless it gives you a great return.

Advertisements in your local newspaper can work well if you are targeting consumers rather than businesses. But you need to give it a bit of thought before jumping in and spending a lot of money without a plan.

We have come across so many small businesses that have spent their whole marketing budget (and more) on advertisements that only produced a negative return. And this happens a lot, although a lot of advertisers do not really know if they are making their money back or not because they don't measure their ads' success.

As long as your results from running an ad cover your costs, keep going. If it doesn't, stop immediately.

There are a number of **common mistakes** made when it comes to running advertisements:

- Small businesses don't aim their ad specifically at their target market. (As discussed earlier, they write for everyone, so no one in the end listens).
- The ad is posted in a paper or magazine that is not read by their main target market. For example, if your target market is women, you would probably not advertise in a motorbike magazine.
- There is no clear Call to Action.
- The ad does not stand out from all the other ads in the paper.
- The focus of the ad is on the business rather than the prospect.

Here are a few tips to increase the success rate of your advertisements:

- **Advertise in a magazine aimed at your target market.** For example, if you are a graphic designer specialising in iPhone application designs, you might want to advertise in a

- magazine that features iPhone apps or industry magazines being read by developers.
- Or if you are a natural therapist, you are better off advertising in health and wellbeing magazines rather than in a general gossip magazine as your target market is more likely to be interested in health and wellbeing and open to different options when it comes to health.
- **Your content, especially your headline, is absolutely king!** Yes, the look is important too. But it is the words that will make your readers continue reading and take action or not.
- Make it brief, to the point and benefits-driven. In the previous chapter you read how to put together your copy easily and effortlessly, so we won't go into details here.
- **Make sure your ad stands out; it's a very crowded market**. Use colours and images that are appealing to your target market. Dare to be different.
- **Your Call to Action is crucial.** You come across a lot of ads that do not even have a Call to Action. What a waste of time and money! You want readers to take action. For example: to give you a call and book in for a free appointment; to come in to your coffee shop for a free coffee; to get 20% off on their next service. Having a clear Call to Action will instantly increase your success rate.

- Here is a great example by one of our clients. Tina, a natural therapist, put a little voucher on her ad saying 'Receive a free, freshly squeezed fruit juice on your next visit when you bring this coupon,' and her ad went from zero phone calls to six new clients in a week, more than covering the cost of her ad.
- **The location of your ad is important.** Try to get your ad published on the right-hand side early on in the paper if possible. You might have to pay a bit extra for this, but it is well worth it.
- **Another hot tip is to write an advertorial instead of creating an ad.** Advertorials look more like an article than an ad trying to sell something (even though they are paid for as well).
- **Images help.** If you have enough space, include some appealing pictures. Photos of people are highly effective as your readers will be able to identify themselves with the people in the images.
- **Frequency is key.** Do not just run your ad once and hope to be flooded with new business. In most cases, this won't happen. People usually need to be in touch with your business name a few times before they will feel comfortable to take action.
- **Always test and measure your results!** Try different headlines and images. Keep improving on your ads to increase your return.

- **School newsletters can work well for businesses that target parents.** They are often very cost-effective. The trick here is to not make your ad look like an ad, but rather make it look like part of the newsletter by using similar colours. Maybe you are even allowed to use their school logo. A good way to get extra exposure and the school's endorsement is to sponsor some of their events and support them in different ways. You will not only gain exposure through their database, you will also gain karma points.

It's your turn to take action

1. Select the right publications your target market reads.
2. Think about your intention for the ad. What do you want your readers to do?
3. Now create your copy following the steps in the previous chapter.
4. Add a Call to Action.
5. Get a designer to make your ad look good. A good tip is to outline your ad with a dotted line and make it appear like a voucher that can be cut out of the paper and redeemed on their next visit.

Test and measure your response rate.

PART 3

Communications and Sales

The language of love

16

Sales

Communicating with intent

"Anything that won't sell, I don't want to invent. Its sale is proof of utility, and utility is success."

~ THOMAS A. EDISON

MATT'S AD REALLY GOT ANNA'S ATTENTION AND sparked enough curiosity to make her send Matt a text message. After a few more texts, they finally locked in a plan for dinner the following Wednesday night at a small Italian restaurant, Pietro's, close to Anna's apartment.

Thinking about what Fabio had said in one of their earlier meetings about 'taking one step at a time,' Matt wanted to make it as small a step as possible. Keeping it on neutral ground and not too far from

Anna's home sounded perfect. Anna got to choose anyway.

Matt was so excited about seeing Anna again, but was also starting to get very nervous and unsure about how they would clear up any misunderstandings. He picked up his phone every few hours to re-read Anna's messages and resisted the urge to keep sending her texts. It was hard for him to concentrate on work. After what felt like the longest few days of Matt's life, it was finally Wednesday. They had planned to meet at 8 o'clock, which gave Matt plenty of time to finish work, go home, have a shower and get spruced up for his date. He was so nervous and excited that he finished work at four-thirty to have enough time to get ready and look good—starting with the hairdressers. He was putting in more effort to look good than a groom on his wedding day.

As Matt was leaving he knew he just had to talk to his Love Mentor. So he popped his head into Fabio's office and stammered, "Fabio... I'm so nervous!"

Fabio exploded with laughter as he saw the glazed look in Matt's eyes and the blank look on his face as if he had just seen a ghost.

"Seriously, Fabio, this is not funny. I need some help. I've never been so nervous in my entire life, not even for my job interview to land my job here!"

Fabio stood up from his chair and gave Matt a big strong Italiano[49] hug. "Simply be yourself, Matt. You have done the preparation. Now just be present for

---

[49] Italians are experts at hugging. Their families are usually so big they get to hug a lot. An Italiano hug is warm, enthusiastic and 'real'.

her and her needs, and remove your expectations." He gave Matt a pat on the back and released him. "Good luck, my boy," he said, sounding like a proud chieftain sending his son out on his first big hunt.

Matt nodded with a nervous smile. "Thanks, Fabio. I'll tell you all about it tomorrow. You know, without you I would never have got this far!"

Matt bought three sunflowers on the way to Pietro's and was so anxious he got there half an hour early. Anna had told him previously that sunflowers were her favourite flowers. To Matt's surprise, Anna walked in just ten minutes later. Matt noticed she had made an effort to dress up tonight. She was wearing a light, flowing, low-cut dress, cute little ballerina style shoes and large circular earrings.

Matt, being the gentleman, stood up, not sure whether to greet her with a kiss on the cheek. He politely pulled out the seat opposite him for her to sit down. "Hi, Anna."

Without saying hello, Anna sat down, saying, "You certainly had some guts to get an ad published."

Matt was unsure how to respond. "Well, I guess I know what I want." He started laughing nervously, not sure whether this was a good or bad start.

"You must be a little crazy," responded Anna, joining in the laughter. That seemed to loosen them both up.

"Without a doubt," Matt replied, feeling a bit more confident but still fiddling with the knife and fork.

"I never thought any guy would make such an effort to get the attention of a girl for a date. It's pretty creative."

Seeing an opportunity, Matt said, "Well, what did you think when you saw the ad?"

"I thought you were crazy," Anna replied, without any emotion. She then paused to find the right words as she peered into Matt's eyes with a serious expression on her face. Matt felt his heart skip a beat. He felt like she was about to drop a bomb. "I liked what I read; I actually thought it's pretty cute and my girlfriends said they'd love this to happen to them." Anna giggled.

They sat in silence for what seemed like an eternity...

"There are some things I need to tell you..." Matt started. Then remembering what Fabio had said about taking it one step at a time, he resisted the urge to say he was madly in love with her and said, "Well, first, let me apologise for the mix up with your sister and for leaving you with Ben. I had no idea Katie is your sister. I felt like a total idiot when you arrived at that restaurant. But she might have told you that I was always interested in another girl. It's just Katie and I got along really well. And as for Ben, I had no idea you left because of him and not with him!" said Matt.

"Katie actually did tell me that she had met a really nice guy, but unfortunately he was interested in another girl... though he had messed things up with her." Anna stopped and giggled. "She said you wouldn't stop talking about the other girl, but she still liked hanging out with you because you seemed honest. And, besides that, she had just came out of a f**cked up relationship." She paused and drew a breath. "In regards to Ben, let's just not talk about that sleaze bag for now. So..."

Matt knew another bomb was coming and his chest started pounding as he looked deep into Anna's crystal clear, blue eyes. "... let's clarify something. Who was that 'other girl?'" Anna was smirking. She knew the answer already but loved testing Matt.

With a nervous chuckle and visibly relieved, Matt, said "Uhh, haha. I think my ad is a bit of a give-away... Yes, it was you. I haven't stopped thinking about you since the moment I met you..." He was about to say more but realised that it was a bit too early to tell her about his feelings for her.

Anna smiled and said, "Well, Matt. I'm glad I saw your ad because, to be honest, I did like you too... before all the confusion started!"

The remainder of their dinner date was spent laughing, getting to know each other and staring into each other's eyes. It was as if the rest of the world had disappeared. Even the waiter couldn't get their orders until 8:30 pm.

Anna confessed to Matt that she had often been thinking about him and that nothing had happened with Ben. In fact, she left the bar on that Friday night because Ben was sleazing onto her and Matt didn't seem interested.

Matt didn't go home with Anna that night but they pashed[50] outside the restaurant as they said their farewells and made plans to meet up again on the weekend.

---

[50] To pash means to kiss somebody passionately. It's an Aussie expression and sentences like 'They were pashing on the dance floor' or 'My mate was pashing some girl' are common.

So what exactly is the difference between marketing and sales?

Marketing comprises all the activities that bring clients to your door, and **sales** is getting them across the line to buy your products or services, converting them from prospects into clients.

Sales are the communications you have with your prospects, helping them make the right decision for themselves. We strongly believe that if you've got great marketing strategies in place, they will do most of the work for you. By the time your prospects come to you, they are pretty much ready to buy. That's why having great marketing strategies in place is absolutely crucial.

Shut Up and Listen...

Being a great listener is a wonderful gift. If you **start listening more and talking less**, you will see a shift in your results, guaranteed. Everybody loves to be listened to (and there are not enough great listeners!). Show genuine interest in the person and aim to help them make the best possible decision, whether it's your cheapest or most expensive item or none of them at all.

If your prospect calls up three different providers before deciding who to work with, and you are the one who is genuinely interested in their needs, they will most likely choose you unless they are price shoppers and go for the cheapest option no matter what. In that case, it would be you running for the hills because as a small business owner you do not want to compete on price. Competing on price will most likely ruin your business. Generally, you can compete on price (don't do it), on quality (go for it) or innovation (good too, but unless you have the budget of Apple Mac this might be challenging). So, the best way for you to stand out and do better than your competitors is by providing better quality and outstanding customer service.

The process of sales should be treated in much the same way that a person would approach a relationship with a potential spouse. You wouldn't meet someone and give them the keys to your house on the first day (in most cases anyway). You would get to know the person and take things one step at a time, building trust in the relationship. Think of your prospects in terms of a long-term relationship.

The best customers are ones that love your stuff, tell their friends about you and keep coming back for more. The first sale is always the most challenging. Simply provide huge amounts of value and do not get attached to the outcome.

"I've Got a Question…"

You should approach the initial sales conversation as an interview. Ask your client questions so you can find out what they really want, and make sure you can give them the best solution suitable for them.

A good measure of how good you are going in the sales conversation is when your client is talking a lot and you aren't. If it is the other way round and your client is asking you a lot of questions such as "How much does it cost?", "What are your different programs?" and "How do you work?", you are most likely going down the wrong path as your client probably does not know what he wants and what to look out for, which leads him to make wrong decisions.

Make sure you are the one asking questions that define what your prospect wants and which of your products or services will be the best fit.

Open-ended questions are really good. They are questions starting with *how, what, why, when…* anything that leads the prospect to talk. Closed questions are questions that can be answered with a 'yes' or 'no' and usually won't help the flow of the conversation, so they should be avoided.

Once you've got your client across the line, think about what to **upsell** them, something of great benefit to them. Selling extras can increase your income exponentially. Airlines do this really well.

After booking your flight online, you have to go through ten different upsells such as insurance, baggage allowance, green miles, hotel, hire car, more leg room and so on that can all be purchased at an additional price.

Or car dealers. They get you on the basic car and then you buy the power windows, cruise control, better stereo, an upgrade on the interiors, fancier rims, DVD player in the back... The thing is that if you buy a $40k car, $7k in upgrades suddenly doesn't seem that much. But if you look at the figure without the $40k contrast, $7k in car upgrades seems like a lot.

Suddenly, this doesn't look that bad...

If you want the prices of your items to seem reasonable, put them next to a high-priced item. For example, if you sold bicycles for $400, you could have a super-model bicycle in your range for $2,000. This will make your other bikes seem reasonable in contrast.

The same applies to the value you offer. If you have a product you would like to sell more of, you could simply put it next to a similar product with less value. **By giving people a contrast, you will be giving them a reason to see an item as a good deal.**

Dan Ariely reinforces the point:

'Suppose you are planning a honeymoon in Europe. You've already decided to go to one of the major romantic cities and have narrowed your choices to Rome and Paris, your two favourites. The travel agent presents you with the vacation packages for each city, which includes airfare, hotel accommodation, sightseeing tours and a free breakfast every morning. Which would you select?

For most people, the decision between a week in Rome and a week in Paris is not effortless. Rome has the Coliseum; Paris, the Louvre. Both have a romantic ambience, fabulous food and fashionable shopping. It's not an easy call. But suppose you were offered a third option: Rome without the free breakfast, called -Rome, or the decoy.

If you were to consider these three options (Paris, Rome, -Rome), you would immediately recognise that whereas Rome with the free breakfast is about as appealing as Paris with the free breakfast, the inferior option (-Rome) makes Rome with the free breakfast seem even better. In fact, -Rome makes Rome with the free breakfast look so good that you judge it to be even better than the difficult-to-compare option, Paris with the free breakfast.

Once you see the decoy effect in action, you realise that it is the secret agent in more decisions than we could imagine.'

We at Basic Bananas would probably just go to both cities and the problem is solved!

Ariely also mentions an example of a breadmaker. When first introduced to the market, no one was interested in it as it was something unfamiliar and perhaps perceived as unnecessary. A marketing research firm suggested the manufacturer introduce an additional model but make it larger and about 50% more expensive.

What do you think happened? Sales for the first breadmaker increased.

Weird? No—once again, human nature. People now had two models to compare, and even though they were still unfamiliar with the concept, they knew that if they were to buy one, they would choose the cheaper one. This one simple strategy made the bread machines sell like hot cakes—or fresh croissants in a Parisian bakery.

So, in your business you could look for contrasts you can create between your different products.

This concept also applies to relationships. Matt, or anyone else, could take a similar looking but slightly less attractive friend out with him to parties which would make Matt look even more desirable than if he was there alone. Might be a good strategy (poor mate though! It's possible that Ben knew these techniques when he agreed to hang out with Matt. He knew Matt was a bit less desirable than him, less funky and a bit less socially comfortable).

Begging for more

If you can get your prospects to experience your product by offering a sample or a free trial, you will fire off what's known as the ***law of consistency***. The law of consistency states that once we make a decision on something, we will make similar future decisions in line with our prior decision. This suggests that a client who buys from you is more likely to buy again. Getting mini 'yes' answers to small questions about your product will benefit you when you ask the big question that will clinch the sale and bring in the money later on.

As with all other methods in this book, this method should be only used with integrity and the best intentions, not to manipulate people purely for the sake of a sale. It is not worth losing your good karma points!

The law of consistency will make it harder for prospects not to buy your product once they have had a trial or made a decision that they are the kind of person to buy from you. The same goes for websites like Ebay. One of the reasons auctions can be so successful is that by offering the product for a low price to begin with, you will get people interested in the product. Once someone makes a bid, they will start to feel the emotions of owning the product and therefore be more likely to keep bidding than if the item was highly priced to begin with.

Psychologists, like Dr Cialdini as mentioned, have understood for a long time the power of the consistency principle in directing human action. The power of this principle, according to Cialdini, even leads human beings to do something they would usually not want to do. He explains that the reason for this is that 'consistency is normally associated with personal and intellectual strength. It's at the heart of logic, rationality, stability and honesty' whereas inconsistency isn't. So we are pretty much trained to associate consistent with 'normal.'

According to Cialdini, the strategy for a salesperson to obtain a large purchase is to begin with a small one: 'Almost any small sale will do because the purpose of that small transaction is not profit. It is commitment. Further purchases, even much larger ones, are expected to flow naturally from the commitment.'

Once you have a customer who says yes, no matter how big the sale was they have made the shift from a prospect to a customer.

Certainty and confidence are sexy...

Confidence and certainty are sexy, no doubt. You are more likely to be attracted to somebody who is confident and certain about whatever they are standing for. If you are confident and certain about what you sell, the easier it will be for you to sell it.

That is why it is generally easier to sell something you are passionate about rather than toilet paper, unless of course you are passionate about toilet paper.

A successful sale is a conversation backed by certainty and confidence.

Don't worry if you are not naturally confident or certain. You don't have to close your shop. Just put in the extra work to know your products and the benefits of them inside out, and then get out there and practise, practise, practise.

The famous author Malcolm Gladwell explains in his book *The Outliers: The Story of Success* that it takes 10,000 hours of practice to master and be an expert at something. He wasn't the first one to come up with this figure.

So, instead of becoming a genius at watching television, get out there and start practising your communication and sales skills by talking to people. Business networking events are a great place to start.

It's okay to be nervous on your first 'sales date.' Just remember that sales are just communications with intent, that's all. The less attached you are to the outcome, the easier it will get. Try it on! The less desperate and pushy you become, the more you will sell.

Excuse me, what are the benefits for me?

We spoke about the importance of focusing on the benefits of your product or service in *Chapter 14 Copywriting that Captivates*. The same is applicable to your sales conversations. Let's look at an example of an effective sales conversation that will mean no more yawning prospects looking for a quick exit, but rather excited prospects who can't wait to give you money.

When we first asked Michael, one of our clients, what he did, he rambled on about the technical side of Search Engine Optimisation (SEO). He was so technical and into every detail that it was like a foreign language to somebody who didn't understand SEO. It was no wonder his sales conversions were very low. People could not relate to what he was talking about nor see why they needed his services. We sat down with him and simplified what he was saying by putting it into plain English and including the reasons why SEO is so beneficial. After putting this into practice, his conversion rate increased immediately. Within two weeks he had sold four new SEO packages. Happy chap!

The more you **speak about what your prospect wants to hear** rather than what you think they should hear, the better you will do. If you are a dentist, for example, rather than speaking about all the details of what you are going to do using your dentist lingo, speak about the benefits of that procedure—amazing looking teeth, the most beautiful smile no one will be able to resist and so on. A visit to the dentist suddenly doesn't seem that bad anymore. By the way, what do you think about a foot massage offered while you are at the dentist?

Tap into your clients' emotions by giving them a big reason WHY your product or service is the best solution for them.

Let's get emotional

In the 1960s, an American psychobiologist, Roger W. Sperry, did some research about the right-side and left-side of the brain and their functions. He discovered that the human brain has two different ways of thinking. The right brain hemisphere is visual and processes information in an intuitive way—looking at the whole first and then the details. The left brain hemisphere is verbal and processes information in an analytical and sequential way, looking at the pieces first and then putting them together as a whole.

Human beings make most of their decisions based on emotions (right brain). That's why successful sales people give their prospects an emotional experience when buying. They make you 'feel.' Why would your wife come home with another pair of expensive shoes even though she already has fifty of those in her cupboard? Her decision to buy can't be rational, right? It is most likely based on emotion. Maybe the new shoes make her feel amazing, or maybe she had a rough day at work. So be gentle!

Why do you go to the one coffee shop every day even though the coffee tastes better down the road? Because the guy in the shop is really friendly, knows your first name, remembers your order and makes you feel welcome. Why do you pay double the price for your dentist's services if you can go to another one for half the price? Because you trust your dentist. Why do you buy a Gucci handbag for $10,000 if you know you can get a similar handbag for $100? Because Gucci makes you feel different.

All of the above decisions are based on emotions and not rational calculations.

It is natural to associate certain feelings and emotions with different businesses. For example, how does Virgin Airlines make you feel? They are cool, fun and reliable, right? We would prefer to buy a ticket with Virgin Airlines rather than another airline even though their ticket might be a tad more expensive.

What about Apple®? Why would we buy all of their different products, even though we might not necessarily need them? Our decisions to buy them are based on emotions. Sorry wallet.

Some people are obviously more left-brained and therefore more rational in their decision making than others.

So how can you tap into your prospects' emotions?

Sell them more than just your product or service. Sell them a feeling, a lifestyle, happiness, safety, belonging to a community. A real estate person, for example, can tap into potential buyers' emotions by walking them through the property and talking about the amazing lifestyle they will have when they are the proud owners of the house. A car dealer can let a prospect test-drive the car and will talk about how cool he looks in that car and how all the ladies will turn their heads when he drives past in his brand new Ferrari.

A life or business coach who is helping people live the life of their dreams can get a prospect to talk about how she would feel, what she would see and what she would be doing if she had the confidence she wanted. This will evoke positive emotions that the prospect will associate with the coach.

Know your prospects' **emotional triggers** and tap into them in an ethical way. Do not use this technique to manipulate

somebody. And again, only sell what your prospects need.

'Wait a second' – overcoming objections

It is only natural for your prospects to have objections when spending money. Some of the most common objections are money, quality and time.

The better your sales conversation, the less objections your prospect will have as you would be already addressing them by asking the right questions that prompt the prospect to talk about what they want. You then highlight the value they will be getting.

For example, if a common objection is the safety of your product, you could ask "How important is safety to you?" Get them to talk about how it's important and ensure that your product addresses all of those concerns. Or if your prospects are worried about the financial investment, you could ask "Is value for money and high quality something you value?"

When addressing their objections, make sure you **speak in their language** and use the words they use. Sometimes sales people get lost in their technical lingo, which can confuse a prospect. Confusion and overwhelm do not sell.

Another great way to overcome objections is the use of **testimonials**. If one of your main objections is time, use a testimonial where a client shares that she initially thought she did not have time to use a product like yours, but since she ended up going ahead she now saves much more time—time she now can spend with loved ones.

The focus of your conversation is very crucial as the human mind is very smart. If you bring to a prospect's attention the things that they do not want to happen, you create a picture in their mind of that actually occurring. For example, if you say "You won't get ripped off" to a prospect, the prospect will immediately create a picture in their mind of what it looks like to get ripped off. So instead, paint the picture in their mind of what they want, for example, "The value you will receive is outstanding". Again, if I say "It won't break" the prospect creates a picture of it breaking, so shift to a positive and say "It will last forever".

Make a recommendation

Don't just sell the same thing to everyone. Only sell what brings the most value to the client. Help your prospects choose by recommending the product that is the perfect fit for them, and give them the reasons why. Repeat back all the things they told you when you were being a fantastic listener—use their language. Too much choice kills the sale.

Where to from here?

When you come to the end of your sales conversation, give your prospect the next step or at least an option. There is nothing worse than the awkward silence after a sales spiel where both the prospect and the sales person don't know what to do next. You've got two options: **Either ask the customer "How should we continue?" or suggest the next step.**

Pushy sales people are not extremely attractive, so if the prospect says that they'll have to speak to the wife or husband and will get back to you in a couple of days, rather than being pushy and trying to force a sale, be understanding and say something like "Great, that sounds good. In the meantime, if you like, I can send you some more information that you could show your husband/wife. And I'll make a note in my diary to check in with you in a few days. Does that sound okay?"

Make sure you then do check in with them in a few days as they might be too busy and just forget about your product or service for a while.

Another technique is **the 'either or' close.** What you do here is make two suggestions to move forward. For example, "Okay, I can either meet with you on Tuesday or Friday; which day is better for you?" or "Would you prefer the blue or the yellow model?" This technique is not giving your prospect an option for a 'no' answer. You are giving them two options, and they are both keeping the sale alive. When using this method, you do need to be careful not to come across as a pushy sales person. Use it wisely and calibrate your prospect. If they need a softer approach then so be it.

Often at the closing point of a sale small business owners become nervous and a bit messy. One of the biggest hiccups, again, is talking too much at the end. When you ask a closing question like "Is there anything else we need to cover to move forward?" remember to zip it. Give the prospect space by holding the silence and letting them speak.

This is not the time to show the benefits and talk about how good your service or product is. You have done that earlier. Your prospect has already made up their mind. So, don't put pressure on them. Do not push for the sale, relax. The less you focus on the sale and the more you focus on the value for the prospect, the more successful you will be.

See this as confirming the sale and not closing; this is the start of a relationship and not the end of one. Beautiful!

You look great

Validate your client after their decision to buy; let them know that they made a great decision. This will help them overcome **buyer's remorse**. Buyer's remorse is when you come home with your new expensive shoes and you start to question your purchase, suddenly worried about the bank account. Or maybe your husband doesn't understand your purchase and you might suddenly feel unsure about it as well and regret it. In the worst case scenario, you go back to the shop to ask for a refund. If at the time of purchase, though, the shop assistant had assured you how incredibly sexy you look in your new heels, you would be less likely to regret it.

It is important that immediately after a sale you **thank your clients** for buying and let them know they made a great decision. **Reward them** for doing business with you. You could send them a card or letter at a later stage.

Do not be another sales person that loses interest as soon as they close a sale. Be the exception and you will be remembered and rewarded.

In the next chapter we'll look at some more communication techniques that will help you increase your sales instantly.

It's your turn to take action

1. Ask your prospects what they would like in a <insert your product or service here>.
2. Use open-ended questions to keep them describing and visualising what they want.

3. Make a recommendation based on what they want and need.
4. Offer the next step and zip it.
5. Validate your client for making a great decision.
6. Build the relationship for future sales. Do not lose interest once they have paid. This is not about closing a sale. It's about opening a new and long-lasting relationship (hopefully). Treat yourself with an ice-cream for a job well done.

17

Communication skills

Speaking your clients' language—love at second sight

"We have two ears and one mouth so that we can listen twice as much as we speak."

~ EPICTETUS

MATT REALISED THAT EVEN THOUGH THINGS WERE now finally pretty good with Anna, he wasn't the best communicator, and he never had been; hence, all the misunderstandings. He figured he had better work on this so he doesn't repeat the same mistakes again with Anna. They had officially declared each other as boyfriend and girlfriend, so Matt was stoked and really wanted it to work out. Once again, he decided to ask Fabio, the communicator par excellence who always seemed to win over clients at work or smooth out any situations his team stuffed up.

"Fabio, you are one of the best communicators I know; you're such a whiz at it. You always seem to win over the clients nobody else can handle." Matt went for the 'kiss butt first and then ask for a favour' approach.

"I wish my wife had the same opinion." Fabio smiled and added, "How can I help?"

"Well, I think I could learn a thing or two from you about communicating. You've taught me all these amazing skills to attract girls, and it's because of you I finally got Anna across the line. But my communication skills are just not very polished. I think it would make a huge difference..."

"You can stop there, Matt, because I agree! I should have taught you some communication skills earlier. The better you are at communicating, the better your relationships will be with your girl, mum, brother and clients—maybe even with your two puppy dogs. Fantastic communicators will never have a problem selling an idea to people, whether it's their wife or a client. Book me in for a meeting tomorrow between 3 pm and 5 pm. Just make it a work meeting as the skills I will be teaching you also perfectly apply to how you communicate with your clients here in the agency. Let's call it a 'Skills Development Session.'" Fabio was grinning like a naughty boy who'd copied his homework from a mate.

"You're awesome. Thanks mate! See you later!"

Marketing and sales are both methods of communication—communication with the intent to attract clients and get them to buy your product or service. Effective communication is crucial in business and can help you positively influence your prospects.

In this chapter we will look at a few strategies that will make you an even better communicator and thus a better marketer for your small business.

What type are you?

The first thing to understand is that there are many different types of people who have different communication preferences. There is no one-size-fits-all.

The best communicators (and you will be one of those after applying the principles in this chapter) have the flexibility to adapt their style to suit the person they are talking to.

We experience the world and communicate through our senses. According to NLP (Neuro-Linguistic Programming), developed by John Grinder and Richard Bandler, there are four main sensory modalities[51] that the human mind can use to

---

[51] Sensory modalities are the channels through which someone receives information and include sight, sound, touch, taste and smell.

process information. We usually have one or two modalities that are most dominant.

The four main types or modalities are *visual, auditory, kinesthetic* and *digital* (gustatory and olfactory are included in the kinesthetic modality).

When you know which modality the person you are talking to prefers, you can adapt your language to speak in their preferred style of language, which will not only make you understandable to them, but also more likeable.

Visual

The highest percentage of our population is predominantly visual. Visual people need to 'see' things and tend to use expressions such as 'Looks good,' 'I can see,' 'I can imagine' and 'Does this look good to you?.'

They often use 'picturesque' words to communicate and describe something, and they also tend to speak a little fast. Visual people make sure they look neat, are well-groomed and are colour coordinated. Therefore, make sure you do the same if you want to connect with them.

Visual people usually prefer to see someone in person when they are communicating rather than only hear them. To explain something to a visual person, you want to show them your ideas and concepts. In your meetings with them, make drawings for them rather than giving verbal instructions, and bring images. Designers, artists and photographers are generally highly visual communicators.

Auditory

Auditory people prefer 'hearing' and tend to use expressions such as 'Sounds good,' 'I hear you' and 'I like the sound of this.'

They often have a more colourful voice with high and low inflections rather than speaking in monotone.

You can also recognise auditory people by how easily they get distracted by noise. If, for example, you are in a meeting with an auditory person and an airplane goes past, they will get distracted by the sound of it. Likewise, a dripping tap will drive them crazy. Better turn that TV off if you are auditory and need to concentrate.

They usually prefer the spoken word (i.e. discussions) rather than the written word. A little tip here; if you are in a meeting with an auditory person and she or he never even looks at you when you talk, don't take it personally. Predominantly auditory people do not need to see you; they need to hear you. Musicians and sound guys are often highly auditory.

Kinesthetic

Kinesthetic people like to 'feel' things and use expressions such as 'I like the feel of this,' 'Feels good,' 'This makes me uncomfortable' and 'Can I touch it?.'

They learn by doing and touching. So, if you sell a product to a kinesthetic person, get them to touch or test-drive it if possible. They will love that.

Kinesthetic people tend to speak and act a bit slower. They generally take a little bit more time to make a decision as they first need to feel it and then they decide. So be patient and give them time.

They usually wear comfortable clothes that feel good. So, if you are inclined to hop into your trackies as soon as you get home (and leave them on to zip down to the local shop) and your partner as a result calls you a 'dag' [52], just tell them, "I'm kinesthetic!" If your partner is highly visual and you are kinesthetic, you might think that he or she is very impatient.

Digital

Predominantly digital people need to make sense of things and tend to be more analytical and 'in their heads.'

---

[52] A dag is technically the matted wool on a sheep's tail, but in Australia it refers to one who is untidy in appearance. They're 'daggy'.

They use expressions such as 'This makes sense,' 'I think,' 'I understand,' 'Can you give me the facts and figures?.' They need to make sense of the world.

Digital people generally speak in a more monotone voice and love numbers, statistics and figures. They learn by working things out in their mind. They like to think things through and avoid spontaneous actions. They usually memorise things by following steps and procedures. So, when you are talking to a digital person, make sure you have some hard facts and evidence to show about your product or service. Ensure your emails are to the point; use bullet points rather than write a whole novel.

What does all this mean to your business marketing?... A lot! **The better you can communicate with your prospects and match their modalities, the more they will trust you**—and trust leads to sales.

In your marketing materials, what you do is make sure you cover all of the modalities as different prospects prefer different modalities (or combinations of modalities). The visual aspect of your marketing materials can be covered by using images. Include some numbers and stats for the digital people. Depending on the media you are using, try to incorporate all modalities into your delivery.

Most people have a combination of different modalities, of course, but they do tend to have a dominant one. The good thing is that you can learn to become familiar with all of them.

Successful sales people are using this information very effectively. A good car sales person, for example, can pick up on someone's dominant modality pretty quickly and then use that knowledge when selling the car. If the prospect is kinesthetic, the sales person would let them test-drive straight away, talk about how good the interior feels and give them a tour through the car by letting them touch everything. If the prospect is visual, the sales guy would talk about the look of the car, how awesome the prospect looks behind the wheel, how stylish the dashboard is, how great the colour looks and so on. If the prospect is auditory, he would talk about the smooth sound of the car when driving at 100 km/h, how quiet the car is while driving and the sound system. If the prospect is digital, he would talk about the facts and figures, how big the engine is, where it's made, safety checks, the warranty and additional features like cruise control and power windows.

A little side note here. This stuff also applies in your personal life. Next time you speak to your partner or kids, listen to how they communicate, how they learn and dress, and try to determine what modalities are predominant. If, for example, your partner is kinesthetic and you are highly visual, you might find that she (or he) is much slower in making a decision because she needs to get in touch with her feelings first. So, instead of getting impatient, understand her way of accessing information. If your daughter is visual and you are giving her orders from a different room, she might not action them as she needs to see you.

Building rapport

You know that feeling when you meet somebody for the first time and you feel like you have known them forever? That's being in rapport with that person. Building rapport with your prospects is crucial as it will create a sense of familiarity, which builds trust, and trust equals more sales.

Based on neuro-linguistic studies, a fast way to build rapport with a prospect is **'matching and mirroring,'** which means copying the body language of your opposite. Make sure it is not obvious (unless you want to be seen as a weirdo). If your prospect is sitting with crossed legs, you do the same. (Ladies, if your prospect is sitting very wide-legged, you don't have to match this, especially if you are wearing a skirt!)

You can also match somebody's modalities (visual, auditory, kinesthetic and digital), and you can match the tonality, volume, pace and pitch of their voice.

If you want to take it even further, you can match their blinking or taking sips of water. If your prospect gets a drink of water or a coffee for the meeting, do the same; it helps with building rapport.

Sounds a bit like magic, doesn't it? Well, it works. Just give it a go. Next time you go into a bar and want to get to know somebody on the other side of the room, just start matching and mirroring them and see what happens. Matt could have tried this strategy when he was desperate to meet a girl.

As an ethical marketer, you use these tools with integrity always.

Big picture vs. small picture

There are people who are very good at details and love talking about details—let's call them 'detail people.' And then there are those who are very visionary and prefer to talk about the big picture rather than the details. Let's call them 'big picture people.' Again, we usually have both these characteristics, but one is stronger than the other.

Detail people are very good at implementing things and pay great attention to detail, whereas big picture people do not want to know all the details. They just want to create big plans and are good at coming up with ideas; though they are less interested in the actual realisation of those ideas.

The reason why understanding this is so important is that the way you communicate should change depending on who you are talking to. If you are selling something to a big picture person, you would mainly talk about the purpose, benefits and the big ideas. If you talk to a detail person, you really want to be prepared with the details of how it all works.

For example, one of our clients sells gorgeous jewellery made in Uganda that supports local women. A big picture person would want to hear about the purpose of the jewellery and how buying them is supporting women and making a big difference. Detail people would want to hear how the jewellery is made and the tools that are being used.

By the way, to be successful in business you will need both types of people on your team, otherwise outsource. If you only have big picture people in your business, you will find there will be an abundance of fabulous ideas but not much will ever get done. You need the detail people to work out the details and make it happen. On the other hand, if you only have detail people, they will just work away and implement stuff without really having a bigger goal or fulfilling a purpose.

A good CEO usually has both characteristics. He is able to perceive a big vision for the business, but also manages to break the big picture down into smaller, achievable steps that can be delegated to the team.

If you are looking for a business partner, it is smart to get a person who is the opposite to you in how they operate. Even though you might have more disagreements, understanding this will help you overcome that. You will complement each other perfectly. (This might be good to keep in mind when choosing a life partner too!)

Storytelling Time

People love listening to a good story. It is something we have all loved from a very young age when we were read fairy tales. We're sure you can still remember Jack and the Beanstalk, Sleeping Beauty, Cinderella or Snow White and the Seven Dwarfs and how much you loved listening to these stories. As listeners, we often identified with the heroes in the story.

Using stories in your communication and marketing is extremely powerful for the same reason. Your prospects will identify themselves with the hero. You can use stories to communicate a message or reassure your client by giving them an example of somebody else that was in a similar situation, bought your product or service and got  fabulous results. If you use a story, make sure it is true—do not fake it. Otherwise, just use a metaphor if you don't have a true story.

As you will see as our love story continues, Matt is so excited to learn all of these new concepts and puts them into action straight away, not only with Anna but also at work with his clients. He suddenly starts understanding certain clients he previously found annoying and learns to communicate their way.

> **It's your turn to take action**
>
> 1. Develop your brand: Have a think about what you want your brand to stand for and how you want it to be perceived, and then develop ideas about how you can achieve this.
> 2. Now let's define your USP. It's an invaluable exercise that will help you market your business more effectively. Write down why people should buy from you rather than your competitors—what makes you unique. Write down everything that comes to mind; this is no time to be humble! Ask some of your clients and prospects too; you'll get some valuable insights.

Conclusion

LOOK HOW FAR YOU'VE COME! IT'S TIME TO celebrate! One of the things a lot of business owners forget to do is to celebrate, which is just as important as anything else in business. When you have reached a milestone, no matter how big or small, acknowledge yourself (and your team). You can also reward yourself with a nice dinner out, taking a day off or doing something you have never done.

If you have had a great year, throw a party and invite your clients. (Even if you didn't have a top one, you can still throw a party). Why is celebrating success so important? Because when you stop for a moment and acknowledge yourself for something achieved, you not only realise how far you have come, you also attract more of the good things because you are showing gratitude rather than just racing through life wanting more, more, more.

Give yourself a pat on the back and celebrate for having read this book (and hopefully starting to implement a few steps). We have covered a lot of great marketing strategies that can help you grow your business and attract more clients. If you haven't done so already, it is time to take action and reap the fruits of your efforts. Our goal for you is to implement one of the strategies covered each month. If you follow the exact steps outlined in this book, within six months you will hopefully have a marketing machine set up which will deliver you with a steady flow of new and existing clients. When you implement one strategy, do it really well, test and measure, and then adjust before moving to the next one.

If you find yourself stuck, learn from Matt and get a mentor. Or join one of our programs, which are also available online at www.basicbananas.com. So geography is no excuse! One of the smartest things we have ever done in business was to work with mentors from the start.

Keep taking action, and as Winston Churchill puts it, **'never, never, never, give up.'**

You deserve to be successful and live the life of your dreams. As you know, business is a never ending adventure, so embrace it and enjoy the ride. And don't forget to share it with others; you are not alone.

We have truly loved writing this book, and we thank everyone who has supported us on this journey (what a journey it has been. To be continued!). We also thank you for taking the time to discover how to become a world-class marketer in your own right, and we look forward to hearing your success stories. You have helped us get one step closer to fulfilling our vision of changing the world for the better, one business owner at a time.

Please help us spread the word and leave a review at

**www.basicbananas.com/
bananas-about-marketing**.

Wait, there's more...

BONUS CHAPTER

to Help You Live the Lifestyle of Your Dreams

A BIG PART OF THIS BOOK HAS BEEN written while travelling around Europe, running and growing our business and living our ideal day almost every day. (Yes, we've done all the exercises in *Bananas About Marketing* ourselves!)

The structure and systems of our business allow us to be anywhere in the world and continue to be paid. We can keep travelling and spend time wherever we want to be. In fact we had one of our biggest weeks in terms of money in the bank while on this trip (almost three months in Europe, one week in New York City and a few days in LA and San Diego). We get a lot of questions about how we do this and strange looks when we tell someone on a remote island in Indonesia that we need to get out of the surf to consult with a client via Skype[53]. We have run classes from the funniest places and at all hours of the night. Ah! The sacrifices you make to live the life.

To be honest, it still baffles us from time to time when we look at the sales we are doing and the flexibility we have. And sometimes one of us will have a moment of "Shouldn't we be at home in the office? How is this possible?" It has taken a different mindset to adjust and believe that it is possible. Don't get us wrong; we have put in a lot of hard work and hours to get to this point. Do not believe it when someone says they have made millions without doing much work or in their undies (unless they have inherited a lot of money and live off the interest of course). It is the hard work that keeps us grounded and appreciative every day. This is one of the keys to the success we have had.

We appreciate everything, any enquiry or new opportunity or email from a happy client. We love it! We are passionate about what we do and appreciate

---

[53] Skype is a software application that allows you to make phone calls over the internet for free (if both parties are online). **www.skype.com**

the flexibility and lifestyle it gives us, and we appreciate people we work with. It sounds weird, but we actually love working, as long as it is balanced with our other activities and fits in around our lifestyle.

We are living our ideal life, but it's not always perfect surf and sunshine. There are challenges to overcome like in any business (or life in general). But knowing that it supports our lifestyle and the lifestyle of our clients is what counts. When we get an emotional letter from a client explaining how we have improved the quality of their business, and therefore the quality of their life, we know we are following our purpose.

Because of the many enquiries about our lifestyle, we thought why not throw in a bonus chapter. We will share with you a few of the systems and tools we use to automate our business that give us the flexibility to work from anywhere. We want to help you to do the same. Depending on how far you want to go with applying the approach, you might have to get yourself a mindset coach or someone to help you to really believe that you can do it. Mindset has played a huge part in our success. In fact mindset and the right tools and strategies are everything.

Bonus chapter from *The Modern Day Office*

Lifestyle working

MATT AND ANNA'S RELATIONSHIP GREW STRONGER and stronger over the following months. They enjoyed true love and passion, and because of Matt's constant personal development they managed to overcome any differences and potential communication difficulties. Even Anna got interested in personal development and together they attended a few seminars. Anna turned out to be exactly how Matt had imagined his dream woman to be. In fact when he took out his 'ideal girlfriend' notes that he had worked on when Fabio first took him under his wing, the similarities between what he had written and Anna were amazing.

Unfortunately though, he hadn't achieved his 'ideal day' yet. He was still working in the ad agency, often working late (not because of beer o'clock), which bothered him now that he had a girlfriend he wanted to hang out with.

Anna loved Matt's humour and generosity. Even though she was not ready to move in with him yet, she was certainly talking about a future together. The thing with Anna was that one of her highest values was freedom, same as for Matt (even though he was ready for Anna to move in). So for Anna, moving in with a guy would be a huge step for her. Plus she wasn't a huge fan of the idea that Matt's two dogs would be chewing up her high heels.

Anna started talking about quitting her job and travelling around the world with Matt for a few months before she was ready to settle down. Matt, who had not travelled much before, liked the idea, especially if it was to be with his Anna. But he didn't have a lot of savings and was scared to leave his job behind. So, he started wondering about how he could live and travel with Anna and still be able to generate an income.

Again, he decided to talk to Fabio who by now was his personal advisor and good friend.

"This time I can't help you, mate." Fabio looked as youthful as always with his silky, shoulder-length hair in a ponytail and his dark brown eyes smiling his usual warm smile. "Look at me. I wouldn't be sitting here if I knew the secret to making money while travelling the world. I would be sitting on a tropical island in my Italian designer swimmers and moccasins, sipping cocktails and painting beautiful women."

Fabio started drifting off into his own dream world. But as Matt was walking out of the office, Fabio turned around and said, "Wait a second, mate. I've got some friends who live that sort of life. I think they have the perfect lifestyle—Franziska and Christo. One of them is Swiss and the other is an Aussie. They set up a business that gives them the freedom to spend a couple of months in Europe, or anywhere else in the world, each year. I'll get in touch with them and ask if they'll meet you for coffee."

A few days passed and Matt hadn't heard anything when he found a note on his desk that said 'Meet Franziska and Christo at 6 pm at the Rocky Café.' And that was the beginning of Matt's journey to living his ideal day every day. There were now many new lessons to be learnt...

Systems, systems, systems

Most of us have grown up with the belief that making money is hard work, and whether or not you believe this to be true does not really matter. If the hard work is done by others or automated by technology, then we can really start to leverage our time and work less hours—but make more money. We have proven this at Basic Bananas where we can operate our business from anywhere in the world. In fact we spend several months in Europe each year and on holidays on tropical islands—and continue to bring in money.

We are assuming that if you are reading this book you probably have your own business or are thinking about starting one. Or maybe you are working in the marketing department for someone else. In the beginning you might have to do the hard work yourself to figure it all out and know what needs to be done. What you need to do is note down all the repetitive tasks you are doing and look at what can be systemised, automated and outsourced.

Leveraging time is one of the key factors for a successful business that allows you to live the lifestyle you desire. You do not see the wealthiest people on the planet doing all their hands-on work themselves—it's impossible. There are not enough hours in the day. Of course, surgeons, orthopaedists and other specialists are successful in their own right. But a surgeon does not get paid unless they are working. They usually can't go on holidays for extended periods of time and still be collecting pay cheques (unless they have someone working for them or selling products). We can't emphasis this enough: Leveraging your time by setting up systems is number one.

You can get started straight away on systemising your business by documenting tasks you do every day. When you do a task that could be done by someone else (most tasks!), make a document or a quick video of how you did it so you can show someone else how to do it in the future. It's almost like an operations manual, but one that will be used and not left sitting in the corner of your office collecting dust. That's why videos are a great tool.

We have our own private website where we have a library of all our systems, documentation of tasks and 'how to' lists and videos. Whether it's something simple like how to respond to an email, or something more complicated like how to extract audio from one of our videos and place it on our members' only website for our clients to download, it's all there. So, when any member of our team needs to do just about anything, no matter how simple or complicated, they do not have to take up the time of another staff member as they can just go to our private website and watch a video or follow a check list. This system also helps us in being consistent in providing the highest quality service.

Video is a great way to record tasks and processes for your business as they are easy to create and your staff members will find it more enjoyable. You can even film your screen if there are tasks that have to be done on the computer. The video files are sitting on our private website and we can give access to anybody located anywhere in the world.

Grow your team

Get yourself a **virtual assistant** (VA). You can hire a full-time assistant from anywhere in the world from as little as $300 per month. The most popular countries for VAs are India, USA and the Philippines. Depending on the tasks that need to be done, you choose where to hire them from.

A lot of those countries have an extremely high unemployment rate, and it is very hard for them to find a job in their country. A lot of Filipinos, for example, leave their families behind to go and work with people in Hong Kong, sending home most of the money for their families to survive. Giving them the opportunity to work as a VA from home is huge, and they are usually extremely grateful for the opportunity and work hard to meet your expectations.

You can get a full-time VA from the Philippines for anywhere between AU$300 – $900 per month, and if you are not ready for a full-time assistant, you can get one on a part-time basis.

A VA can do anything for you that does not require them being physically in the country. Most administrative and repetitive tasks can be done from anywhere; even phone calls can be outsourced. Just make sure your assistants speak your clients' language really well. Don't follow the example of telcos whose callers are often based in India and hard to understand.

Creating your 'how to' videos is the perfect way to train your VA and make sure things are done the way you want them to be. We create new videos all the time as we improve the way we do things, and now our VAs are also creating videos when they are doing a repetitive task. So, whenever we need a new team member, the videos are fabulous staff training tools.

You can of course also get a VA in your own country. There are many fabulous VAs in Australia, for example, who offer some excellent services. We employ a range of people and contract workers in Australia, the USA, Canada and the Philippines depending on the required skill set.

How do you get started with a VA?

First, keep a diary of what you do with your time. Create a simple spreadsheet showing each day of the week and make a note of everything you do each hour for a whole month. This will show you exactly which repetitive tasks you are doing and what can be outsourced.

After a month, review your lists and highlight the repetitive tasks that can be outsourced and the ones you can create a system for.

Make a document or video of how you do the tasks next time you do them, and you are on your way to creating your own operations manual. This will be the basis for you to train your staff. It will also help your VA to know how to complete tasks, plus it will give you direction in what skills you need to look for when hiring a VA.

Do the math. If you work for $60 per hour and you can outsource work to someone you pay $30 per hour or less, then you are coming out in front. Keep doing what makes you $60 per hour and let the other tasks be done by others. The output of your business should then increase and start to generate more income.

"Shouldn't I do it myself to make more money?" We get this question a lot, and if you are in a situation where you have time to do extra work yourself then you can do so. But if you want rapid business growth, you need to focus your extra hours on marketing your business to attract more clients and keep the existing ones happy. Most business owners don't have a spare minute in the day, but they are happy to do more work. It's either a fear of losing control, worry that others won't do the work right, or a fear of spending money on someone else. They do not see spending a little money on someone else as an investment to free up their own time to allow them to focus on bigger things, or as a way to generate more sales.

If you are doing tasks you do not enjoy then they are the first ones you should outsource (except for your marketing and finances). Tasks that can be outsourced are administration, bookkeeping, website updating, graphic design, answering your phone and cleaning.

The fulfillment of your product can be outsourced as well, using a fulfillment company (also called a fulfillment house). If you provide a product (almost any kind), there's no need to rent a warehouse, pay all the costs involved or deal with the headaches.

For us, working from anywhere has meant that a fulfillment company is a must. We can be working from a beach in Spain or searching for surf in Indonesia and know that resources including CDs, newsletters, documents and templates will be sent to our clients on the exact dates they are due. Our fulfillment company is looking after it all for us while we are off doing other things.

If you are running your own micro business and you are alone, it is especially crucial that you focus on marketing and sales. Most small and micro business owners should be spending the majority of their time on these income-generating activities. Once you are making money, then you can tidy up other areas of your business.

Automation

Automate wherever possible. The only thing that's better than outsourcing to a human is outsourcing to software or a program. It might not be good for creating jobs, but it's good for business, and if you allow your business to grow (through systems and automation), you will automatically create jobs. (It's still better than sitting on the couch doing nothing, right?) Small businesses are the lifeblood of the economy, so we need to strengthen that sector and decrease the rate of small business failure (a huge topic!).

For example, if you are an accountant and you send a tax reminder to your clients, this can be automated so you know the right content is sent every time without you having to sit there and click 'send' for every client.

If you are a plumber, you could automate a 'Thank you' card after every job and set up a series of follow-up emails that go to your past customers to say hi every month. This will remind them that you are there and ensure they have your contact details on hand.

Emails are just one example of automating certain aspects. There are lots of programs and software that can automate your business. These systems can also do the marketing for you so you can concentrate on other things, plus avoid human mistakes.

There are so many things you can do to grow your business and create more freedom and time for yourself and your family...

Now it's time to implement the things we've covered... Keep implementing every day and remember, it's all the little things that you do that add up to make a big impact...

More products and programs by the authors

Blast-Off Marketing Workshop

IN THIS SHORT, JAM-PACKED WORKSHOP the Basic Bananas team pull back the curtains on the most effective ways to attract clients. The fastest way to grow your business is to use clever marketing! The good news is that it's not really rocket science, but there are a few key elements you must know to avoid a scattered approach to marketing. *Marketing Blast-Off* is an intensive half-day workshop where you will discover the steps to make your business stand out from the crowd, attract new clients, and add more money to the bottom line.

These workshops are available globally. Please visit **www.basicbananas.com/blast-off** to find the nearest location!

The Online Eco System – FREE Online Marketing Course

This program demystifies online marketing for business owners. Discover the online eco-system to create online marketing campaigns for your business.

This is a free step-by-step course, which will guide you to take your online marketing to a whole new level.

Access this program here:

www.basicbananas.com/ecosystem

Subscribe to Basic Bananas Radio

Every week, the founders of Basic Bananas release a new radio episode you can access via iTunes. The show delivers nothing but extremely valuable tips and tricks specifically for small business owners. Open your podcast App, search for Basic Bananas and hit subscribe.

The Clever Bunch Program

The Clever Bunch is a step-by-step twelve months program with monthly live workshops to create a marketing machine that brings in a constant flow of clients.

Learn more at

www.basicbananas.com/cleverbunch

The Marketing Smarts

The Marketing Smarts is an online training and mentoring program to grow your business, using a combination of online and offline marketing strategies.

Check it out at

www.themarketingsmarts.com

About the authors

FRANZISKA AND CHRISTO ARE INSPIRING entre-preneurs, speakers, authors and the founders of Basic Bananas – Small Business Marketing Made Simple. Through their thriving business they are helping thousands of small business owners grow their businesses year after year and live the lifestyle of their dreams.

They have turned on its head the status quo on how to run a business and have created and grown a business to support their ideal lifestyle, and not the other way around. And they are doing the same for their clients.

Franziska and Christo are on a mission to support business owners worldwide, changing the way people do business to make it more empowering for both the business owner and their clients.

They are also big believers in social business, making a difference through entrepreneurship, and are supporting various projects locally and in the Third World.

As well as their passion for business, Franziska and Christo love surfing, travelling, playing music, spending time with friends and family, and undertaking all sorts of adventures.

Franziska Iseli

Franziska Iseli is a maverick entrepreneur, leading marketing and brand strategist, speaker, author and the co-founder of BasicBananas.com, OceanLovers.global, YoursSocially.com, TheBusinessHood.com and Impacteurs.com.

In 2013 Franziska was awarded the Young Entrepreneur of the Year Award recognizing her innovation, creativity, and philanthropic involvement.

A true visionary, no challenge seems to be too big for Franziska. She is known for her rebellious nature and challenging the norm. She has this rare combination of being both creative and strategic, which makes her a powerful thought leader in the business world.

The key to Franziska's success is her down-to-earth attitude, infectious energy, integrity, and fearlessness to take the lead. As a Swiss-born Aussie with a sharp-witted humor, and the ability to speak five languages, she has also been known to make up a few words.

Franziska is a big believer in social business and is always on the lookout for social projects; the latest ones include the adoption of a Mongolian wild horse and a whale.

To find out more visit **franziskaiseli.com** or connect with her via different social media channels **@franziskaiseli**.

Christo Hall

Christo Hall is a clever entrepreneur, online marketing strategist, speaker, author, and the co-founder of BasicBananas.com and TheBusinessHood.com

When it comes to innovative marketing tips and tricks to attract new business, Christo is the man. He has helped thousands of business owners to create powerful strategies, add millions in additional income, and build scalable marketing systems.

Christo has always been very entrepreneurial. He claims to never have had a 'real' job and he learned how to make money and appeal to customers at a young age. After being a full-time professional surfer for eight years, he became a full-time entrepreneur (working part time) and hasn't looked back since.

Christo is known for his out-of-the-box thinking and leadership, and doesn't play by the rules of convention.

Franziska and Christo are world-renowned speakers and regularly present at some of the largest conferences around the globe including TEDx. Their advice is regularly sought by the media and they have been featured across different publications including the Sydney Morning Herald, The Huffington Post, Channel 9, BRW, Virgin Inflight Radio and 2UE.

To book them for your next event, please visit **www.franziskaandchristo.com**.

References

1. D Ariely, *Predictably Irrational*, Harper Collins Publishers, New York, NY, 2010.
2. Dr. R Cialdini, *Influence: The Psychology of Persuasion*, Harper Business; New York, NY, Rev. Ed., 2006.
3. M Gladwell, *The Outliers: The Story of Success*, Hachette Book Group, New York, NY, 2011.
4. C Hopkins, *My Life in Advertising*, Palmera Publishing, 2012.
5. S Jeffers, *Feel the fear and do it anyway*, Ebury Publishing, Random House, UK,. 2007.
6. A Robbins, *Awaken the Giant Within-How to take control of your mental, emotional, physical and financial destiny*, Free Press (Simon & Schuster), New York, NY, 1992.
7. J Vitale, *Hypnotic Writing*, John Wiley & Sons, Hoboken, NJ, 2006.

www.ingramcontent.com/pod-product-compliance
Lightning Source LLC
Chambersburg PA
CBHW070050080526
44586CB00013B/993